# SWEARY MARY & HER FRIENDS

**Tell It Like It Is!**

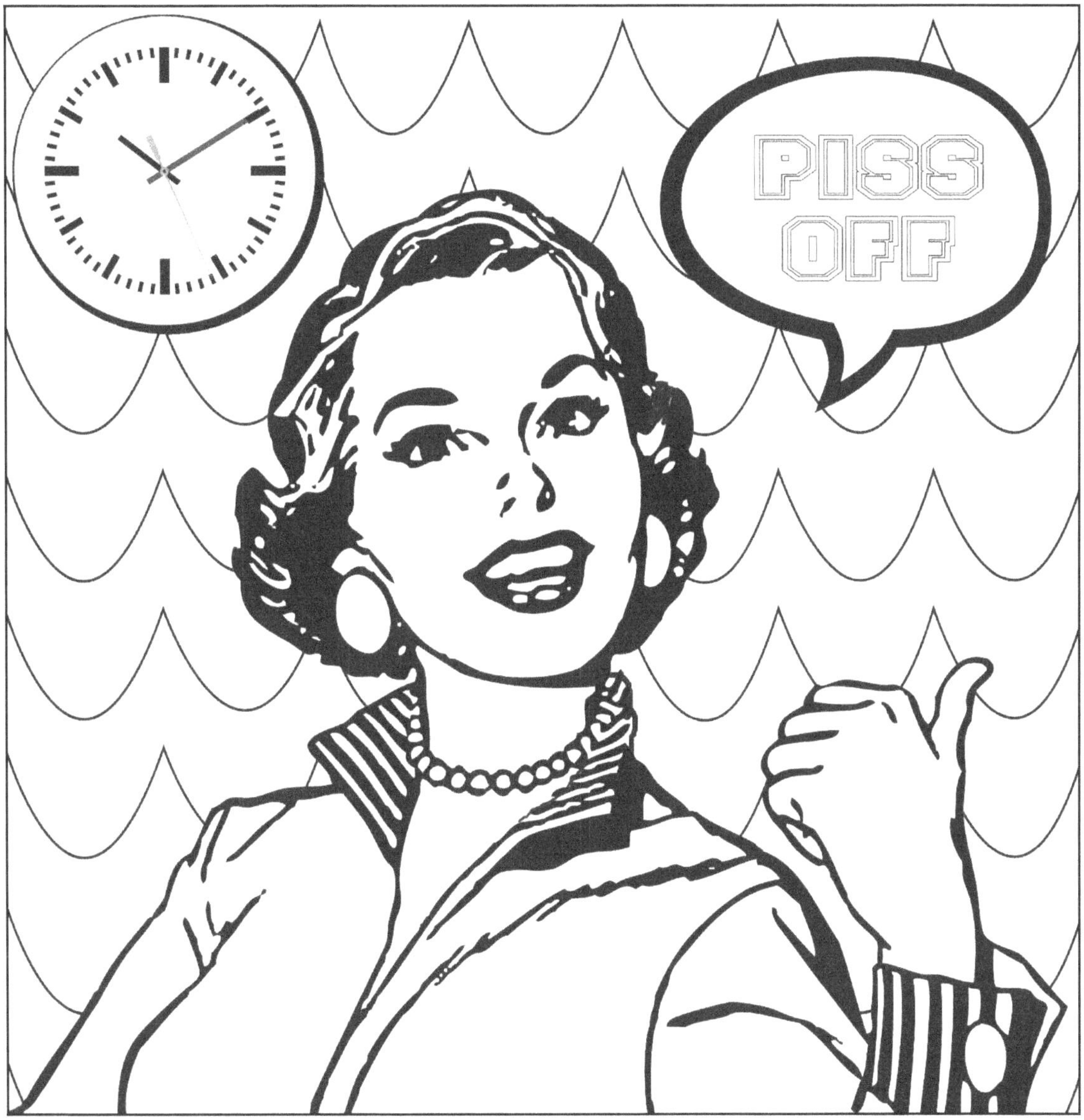


**Adult Swear Word Coloring Book**

PARENTAL
ADVISORY
EXPLICIT CONTENT

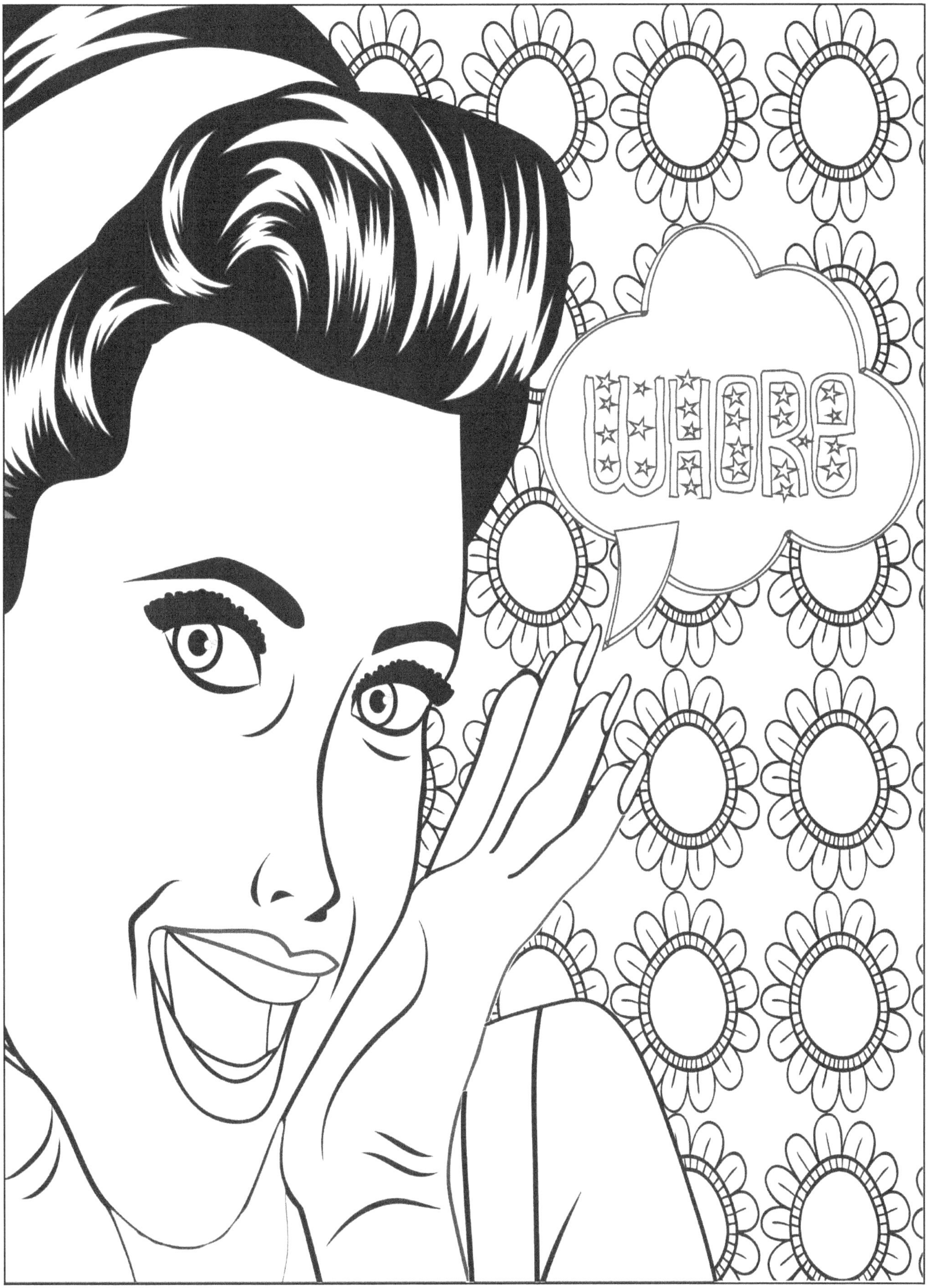
WHORE

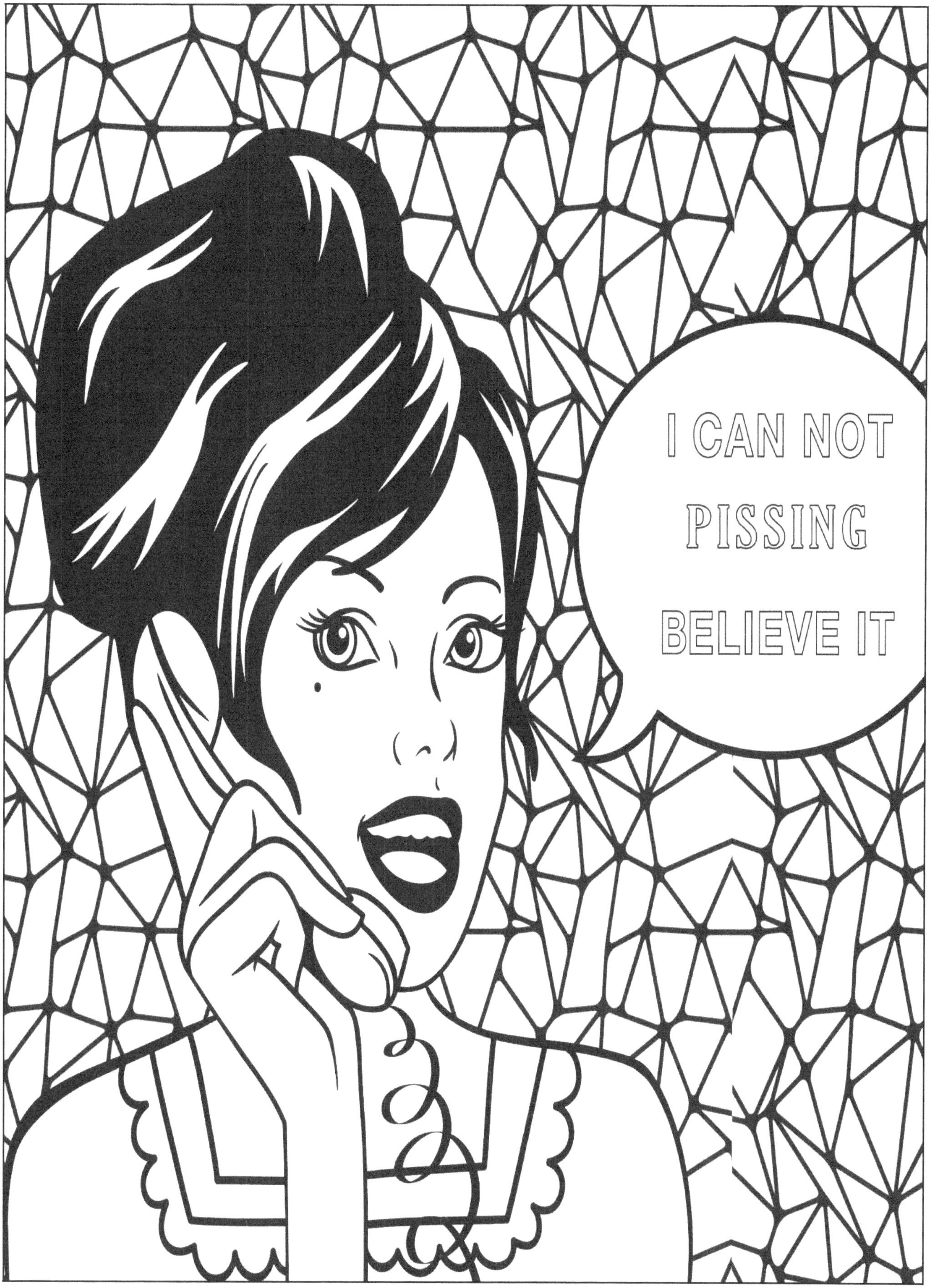
I CAN NOT
PISSING
BELIEVE IT

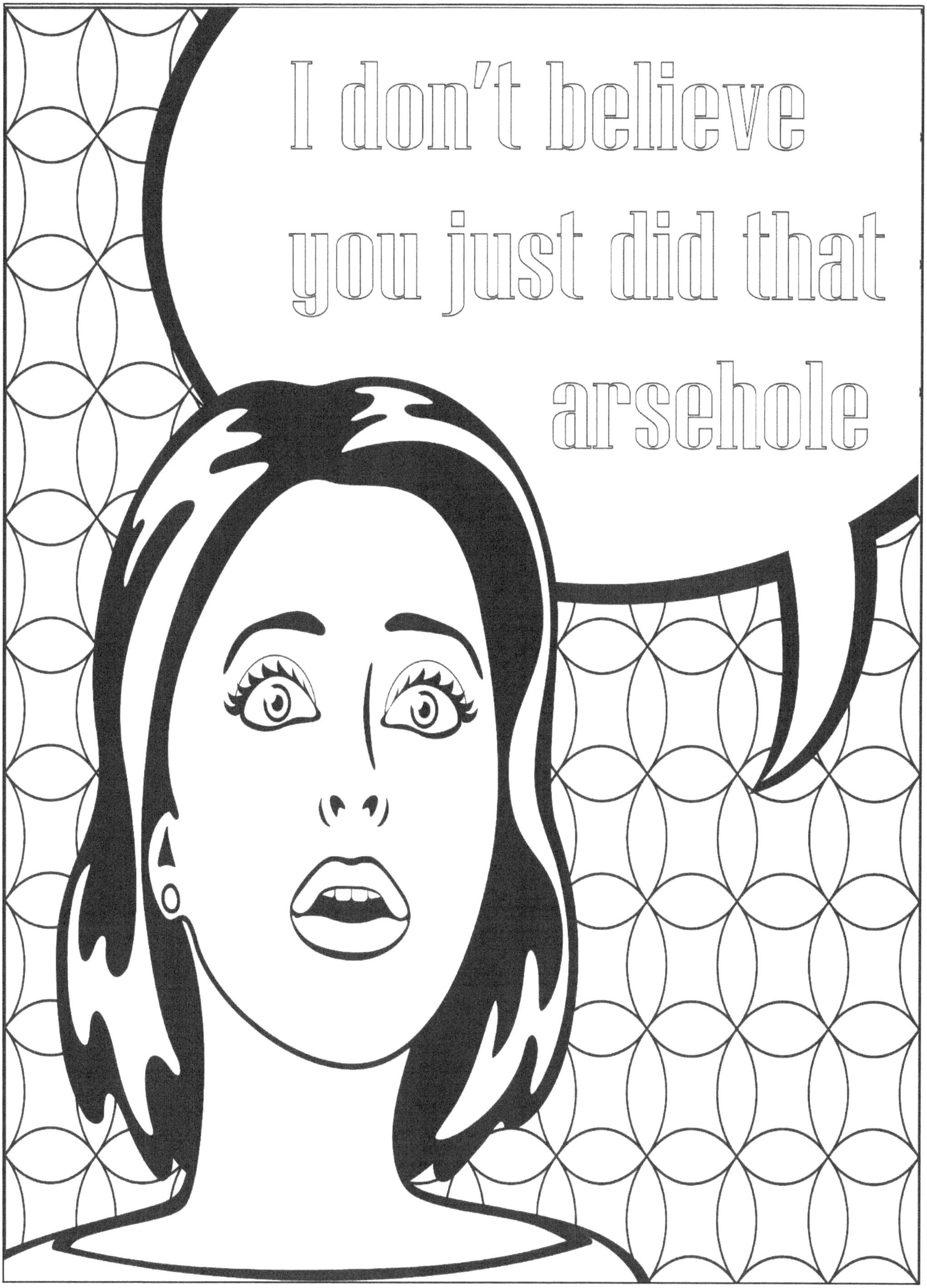
I don't believe you just did that arsehole

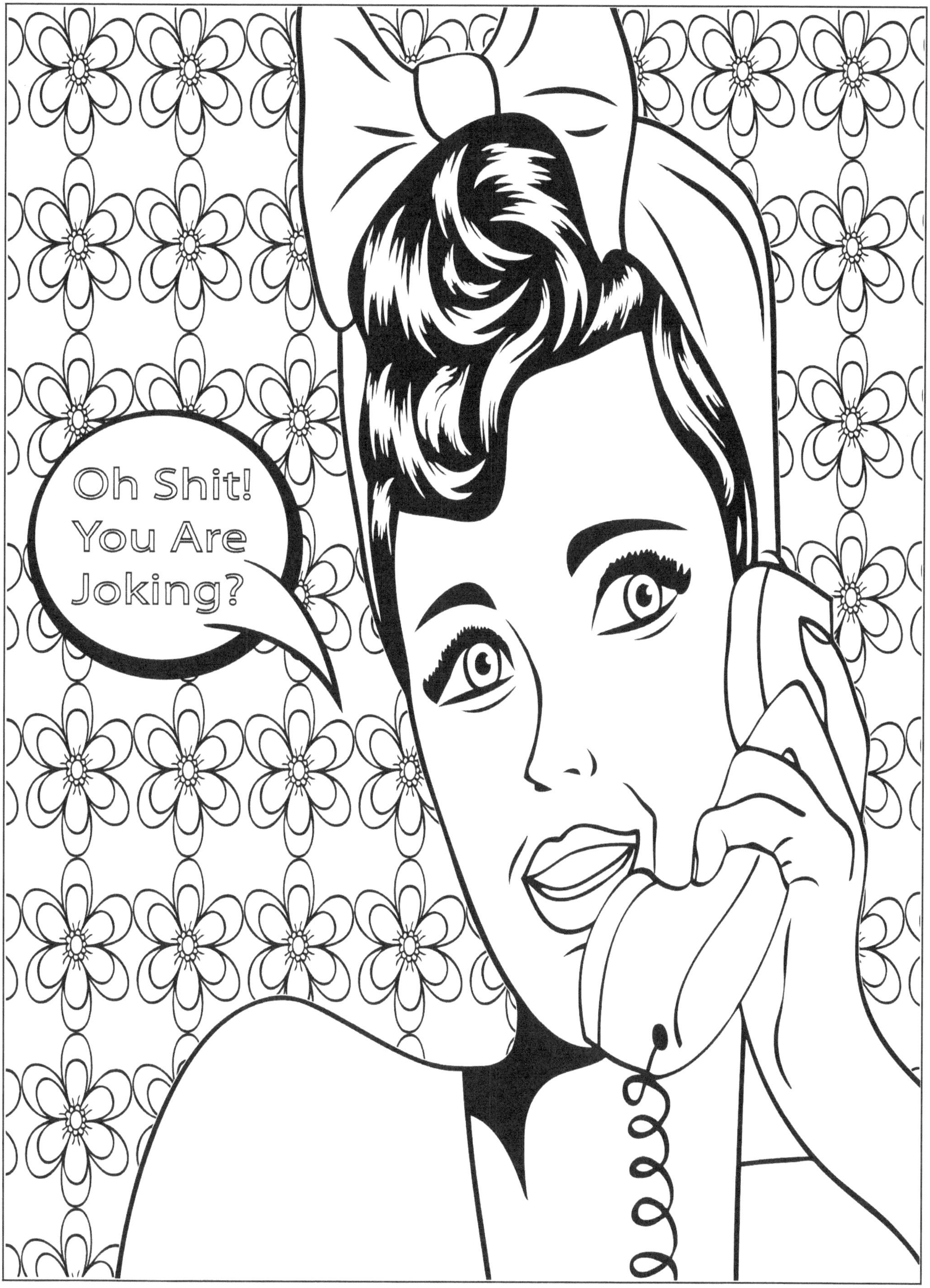
Oh Shit!
You Are
Joking?

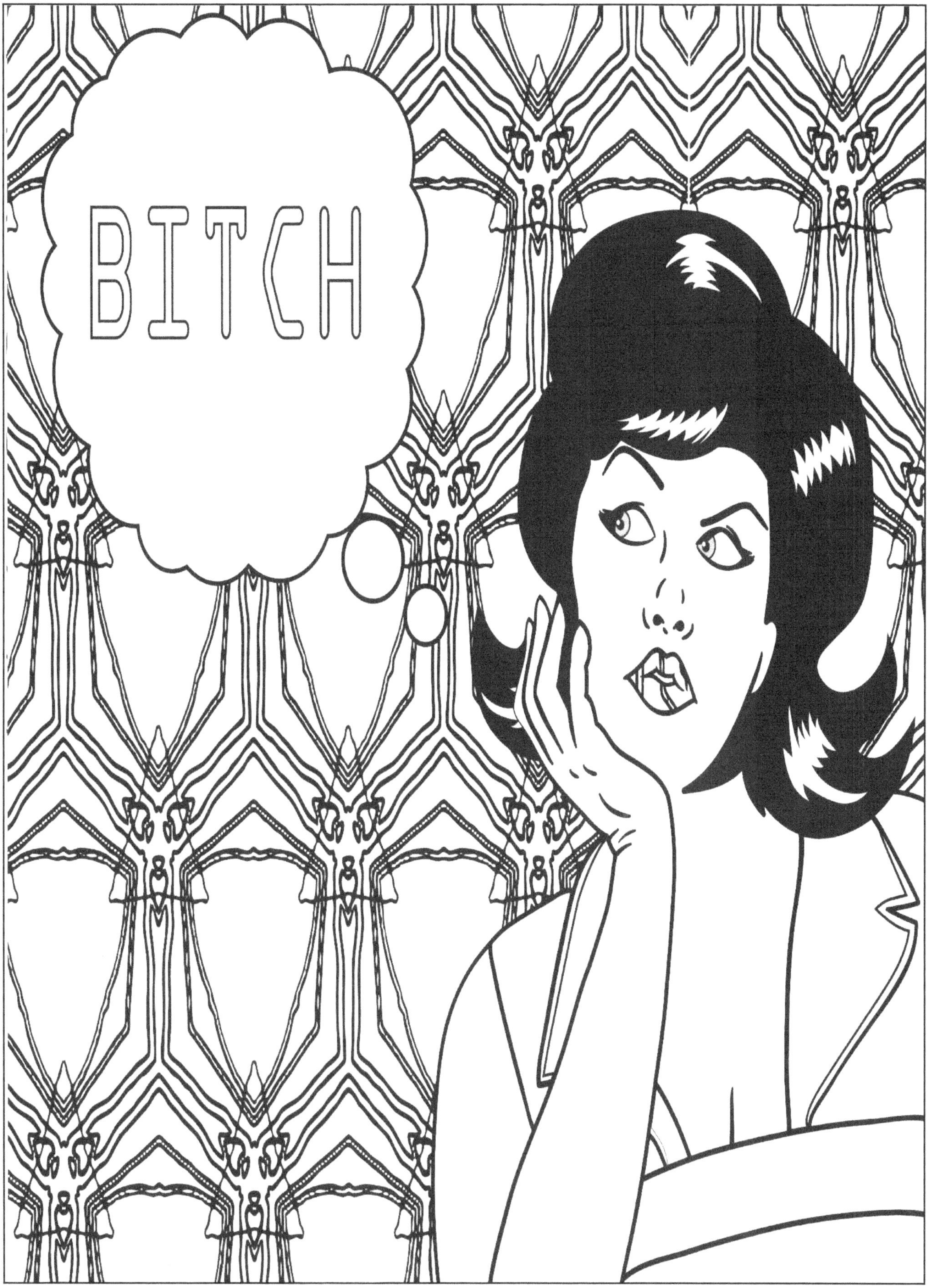
BITCH

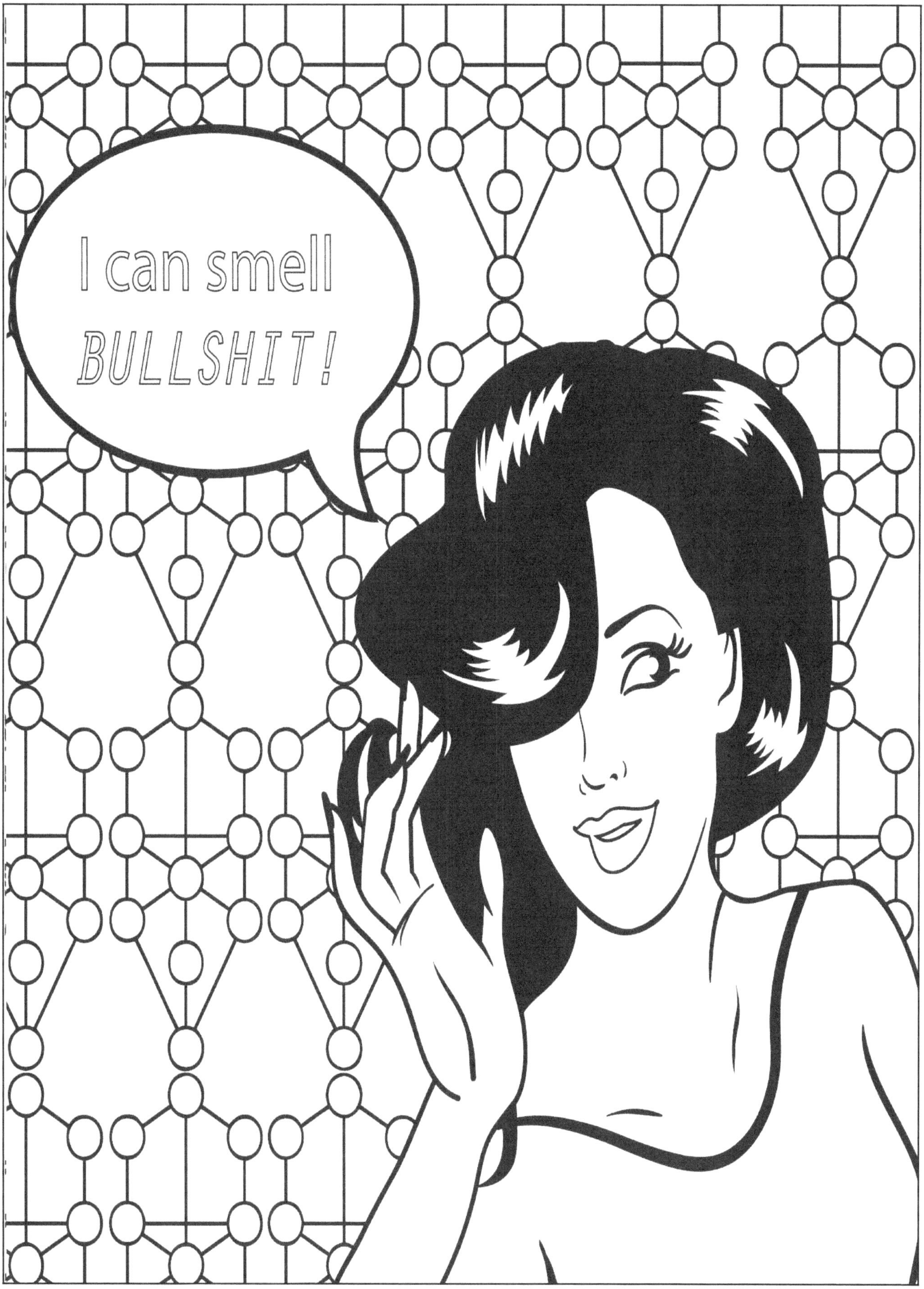
I can smell
BULLSHIT!

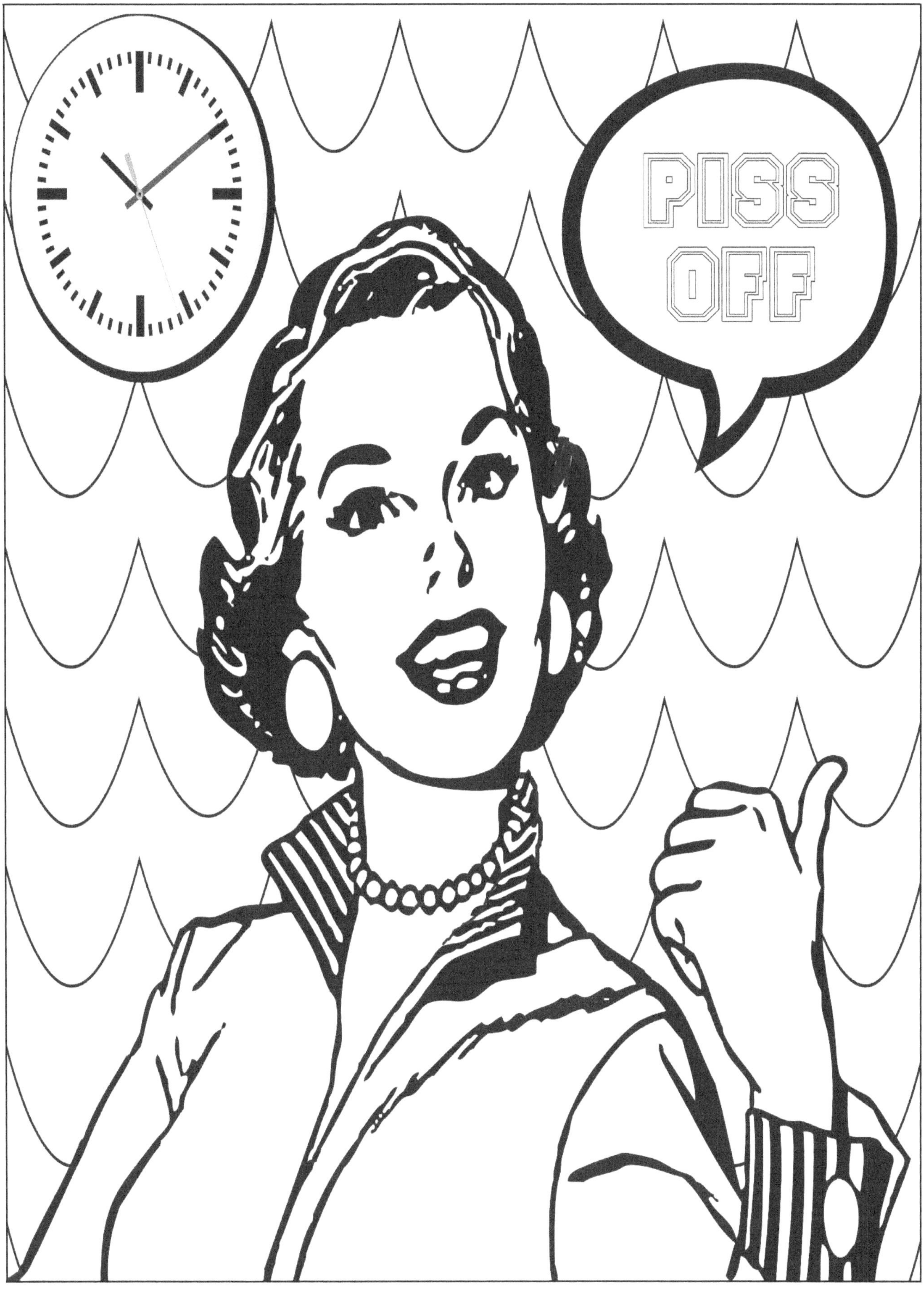
PISS
OFF

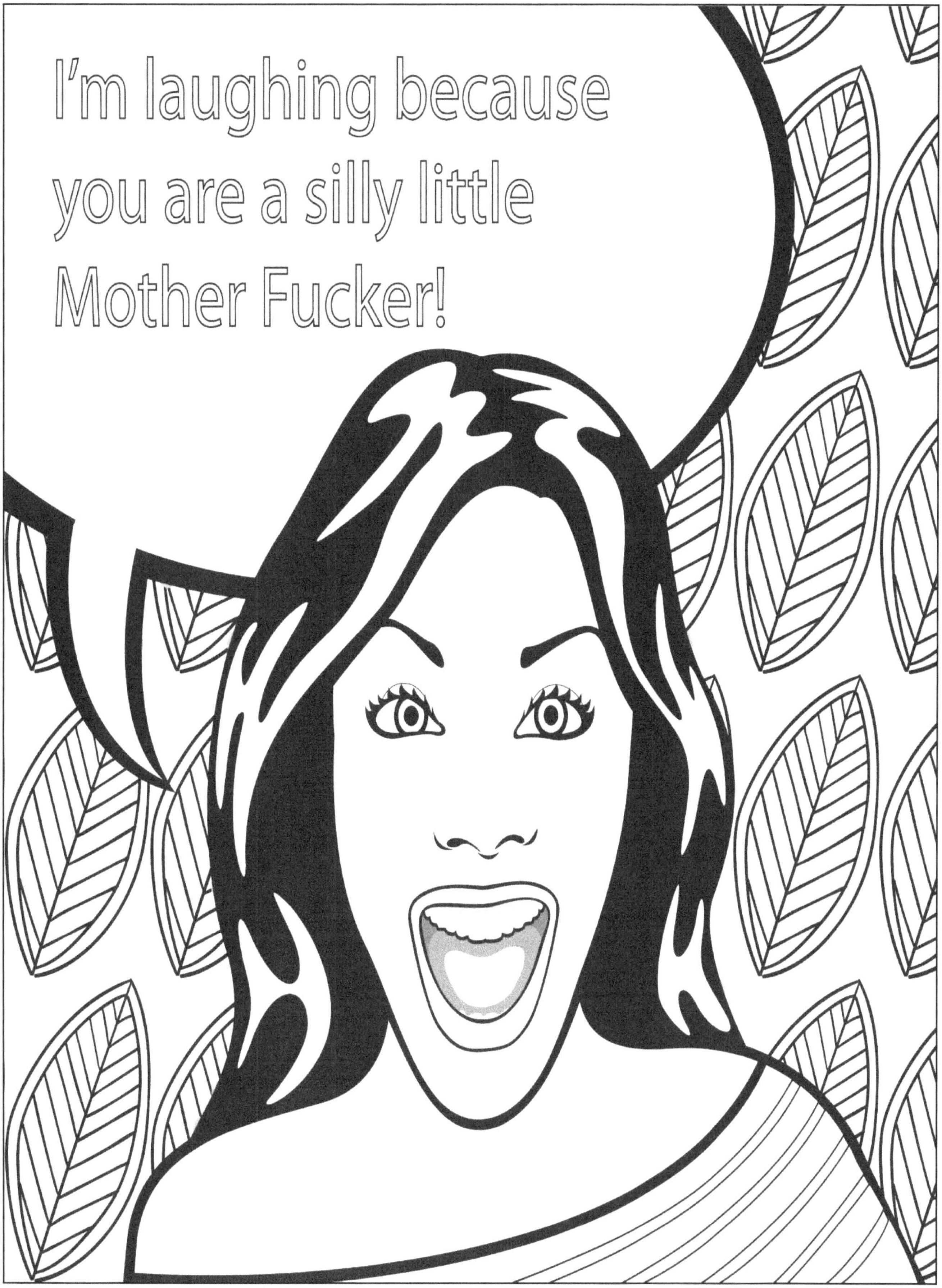
I'm laughing because you are a silly little Mother Fucker!

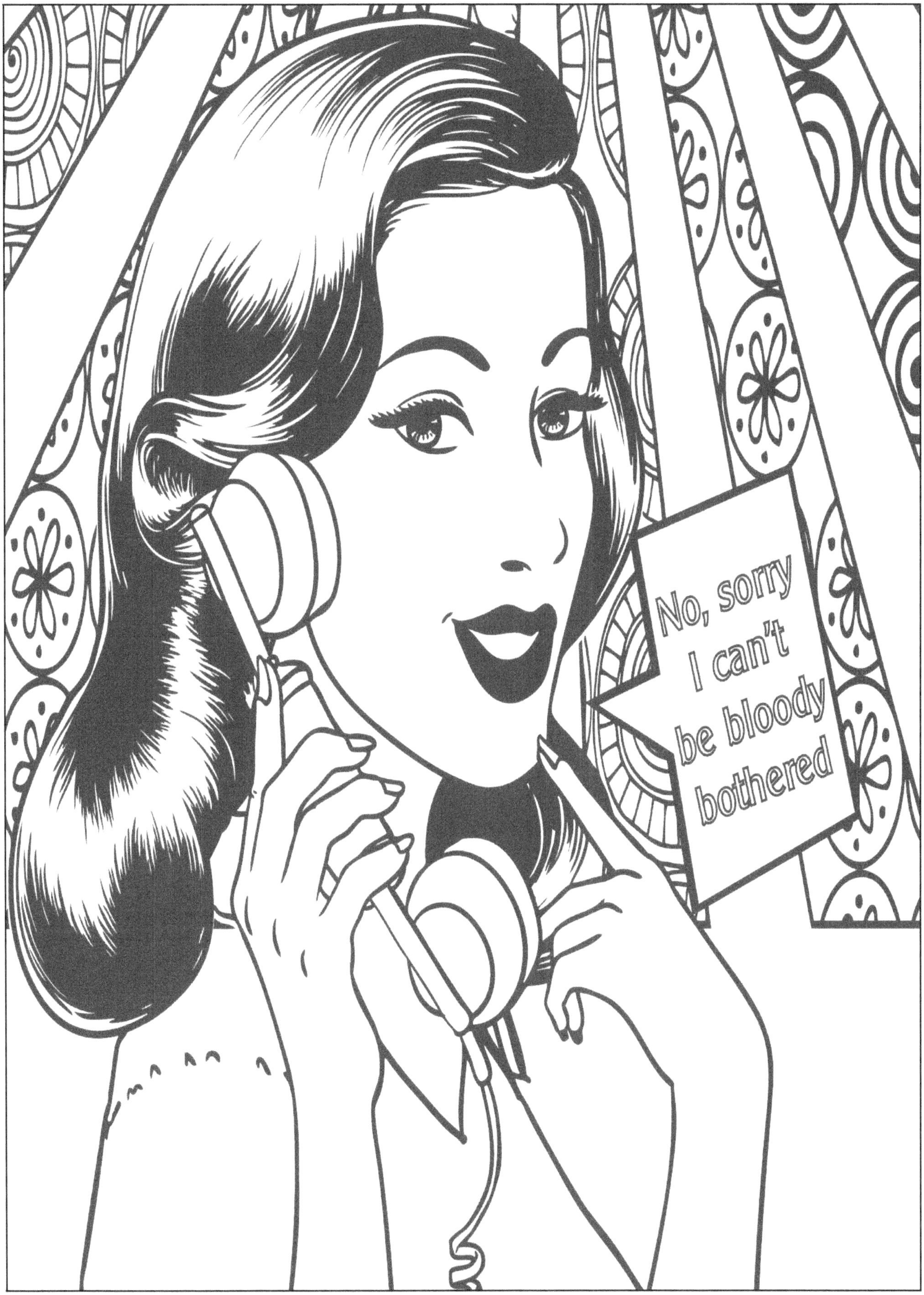
No, sorry I can't be bloody bothered

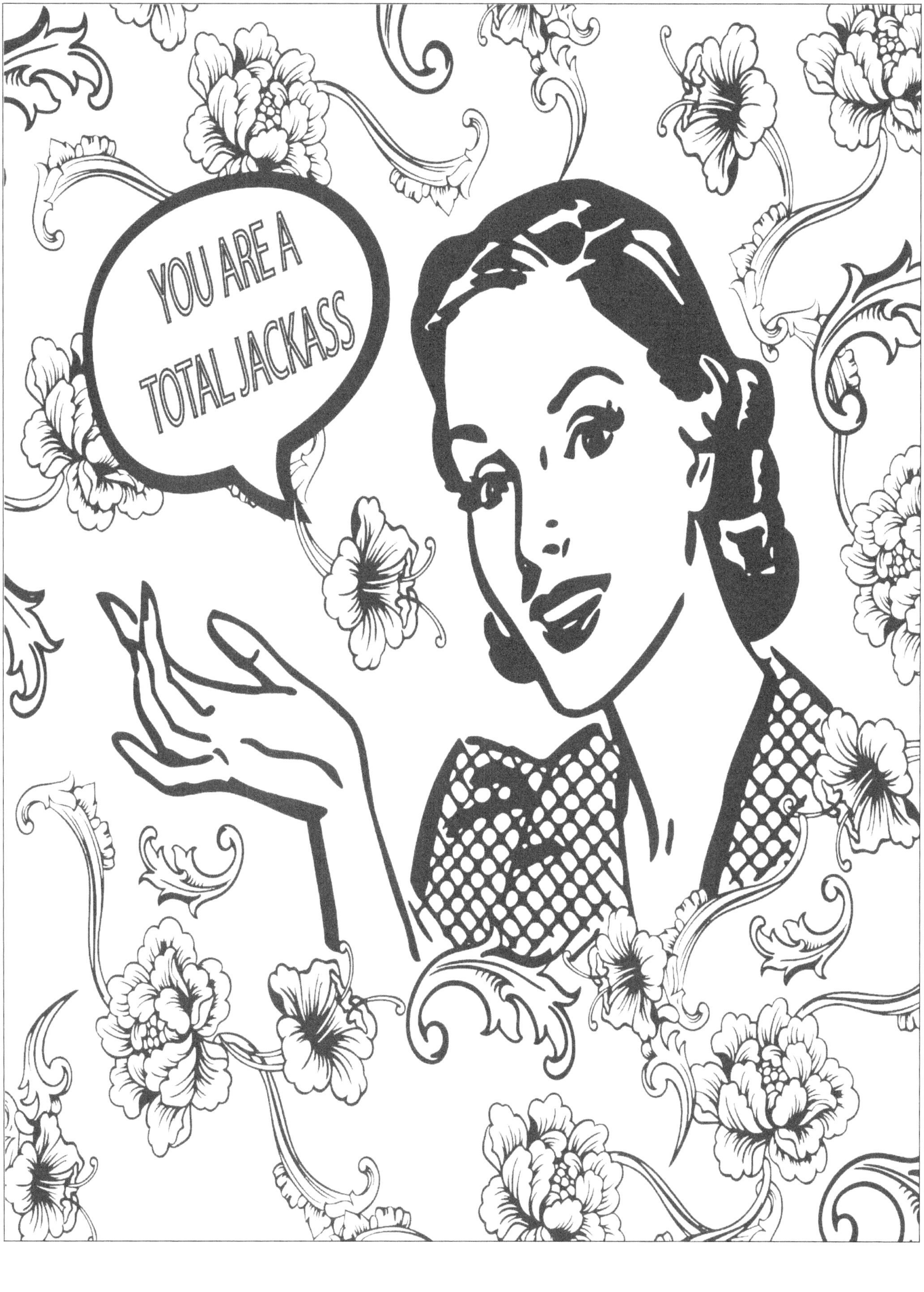
YOU ARE A TOTAL JACKASS

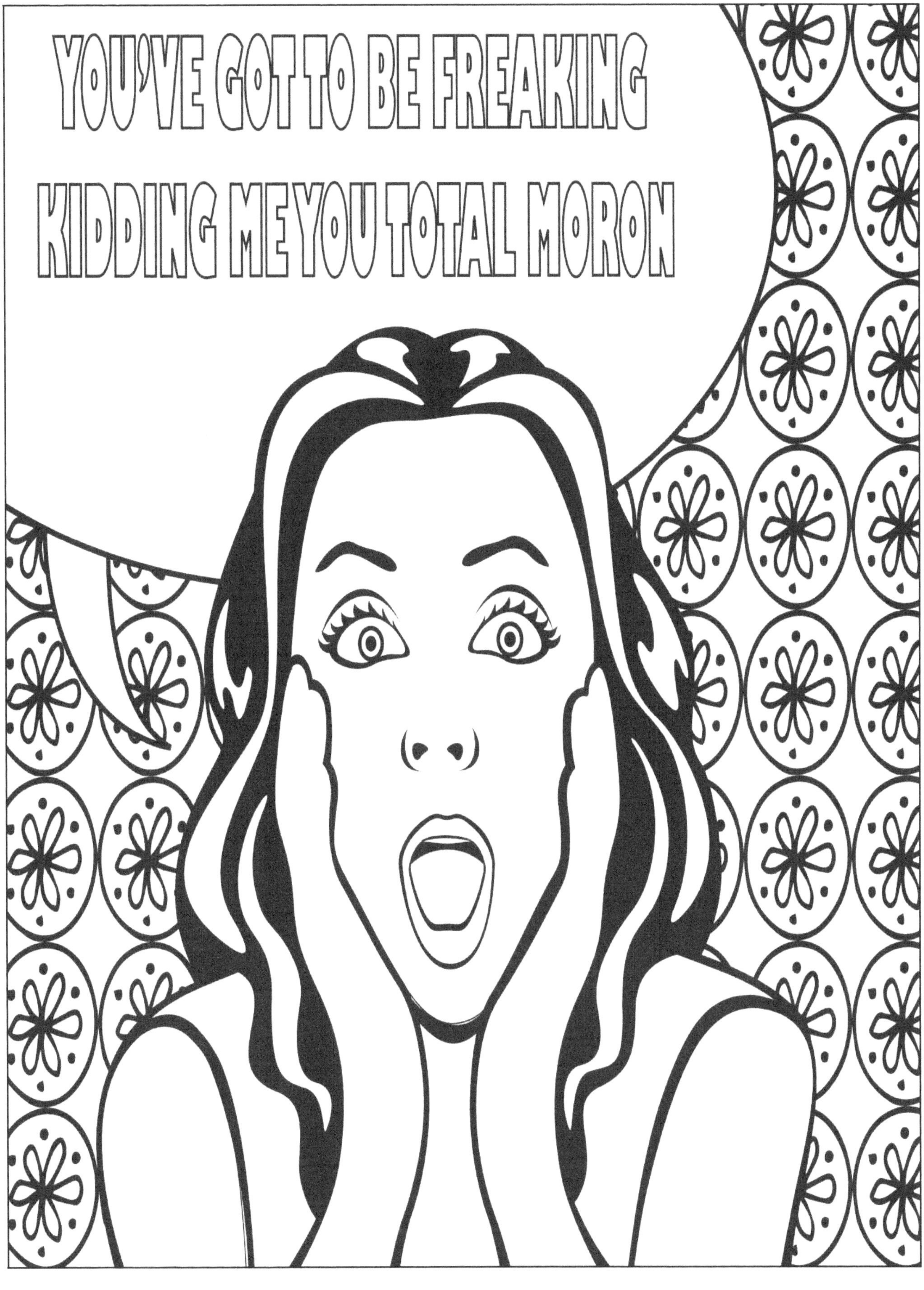
YOU'VE GOT TO BE FREAKING
KIDDING ME YOU TOTAL MORON

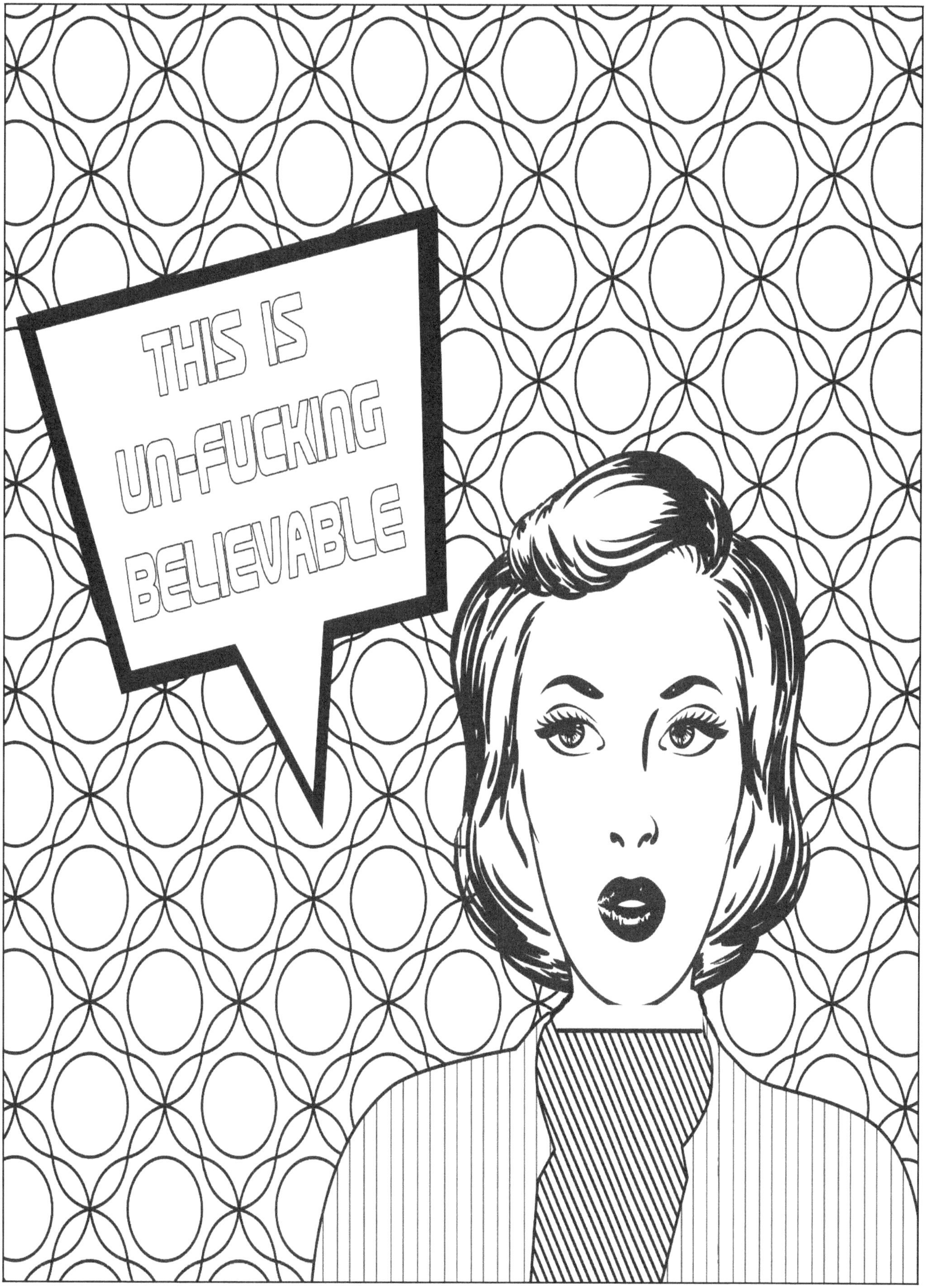
THIS IS
UN-FUCKING
BELIEVABLE

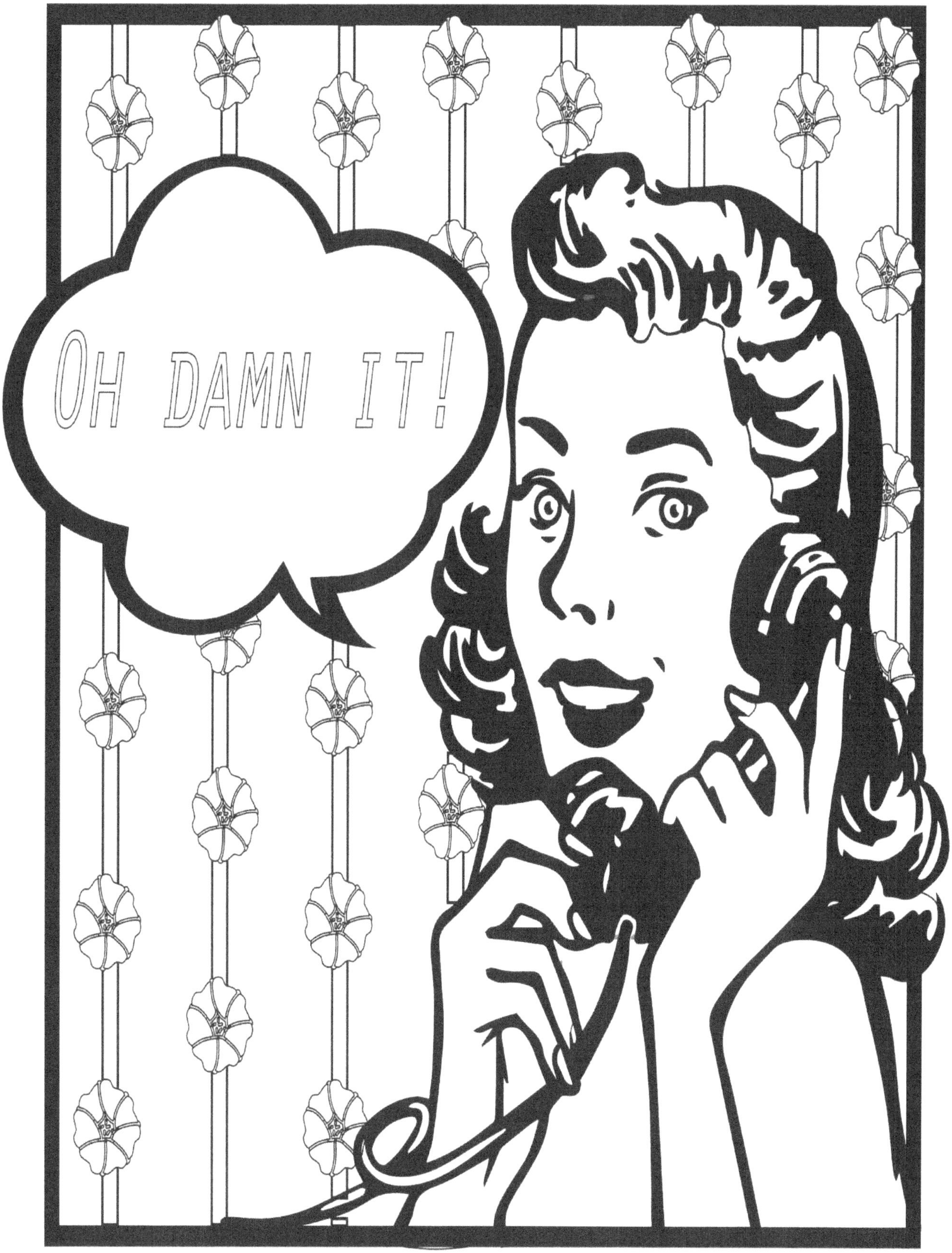
OH DAMN IT!

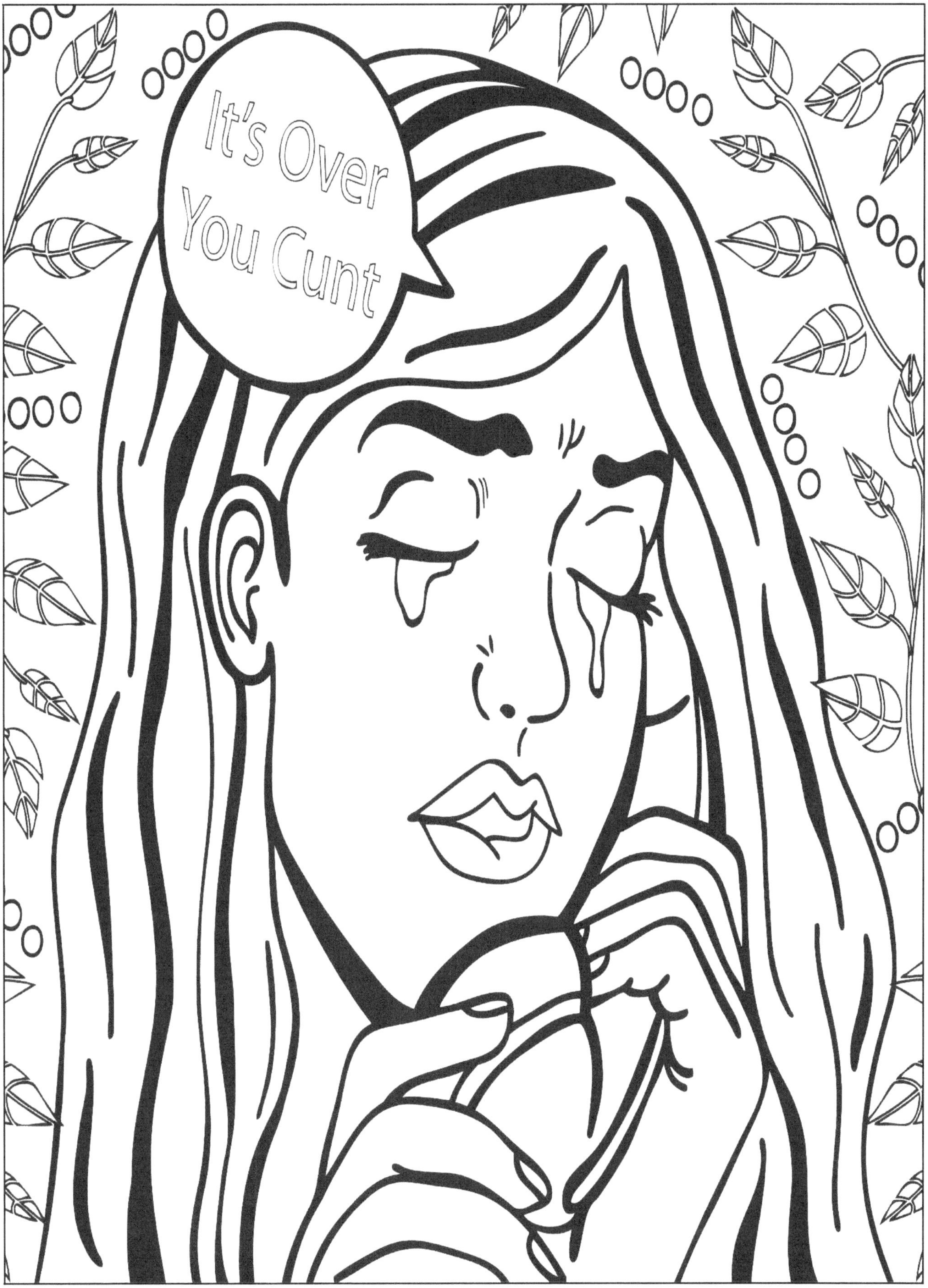
It's Over You Cunt

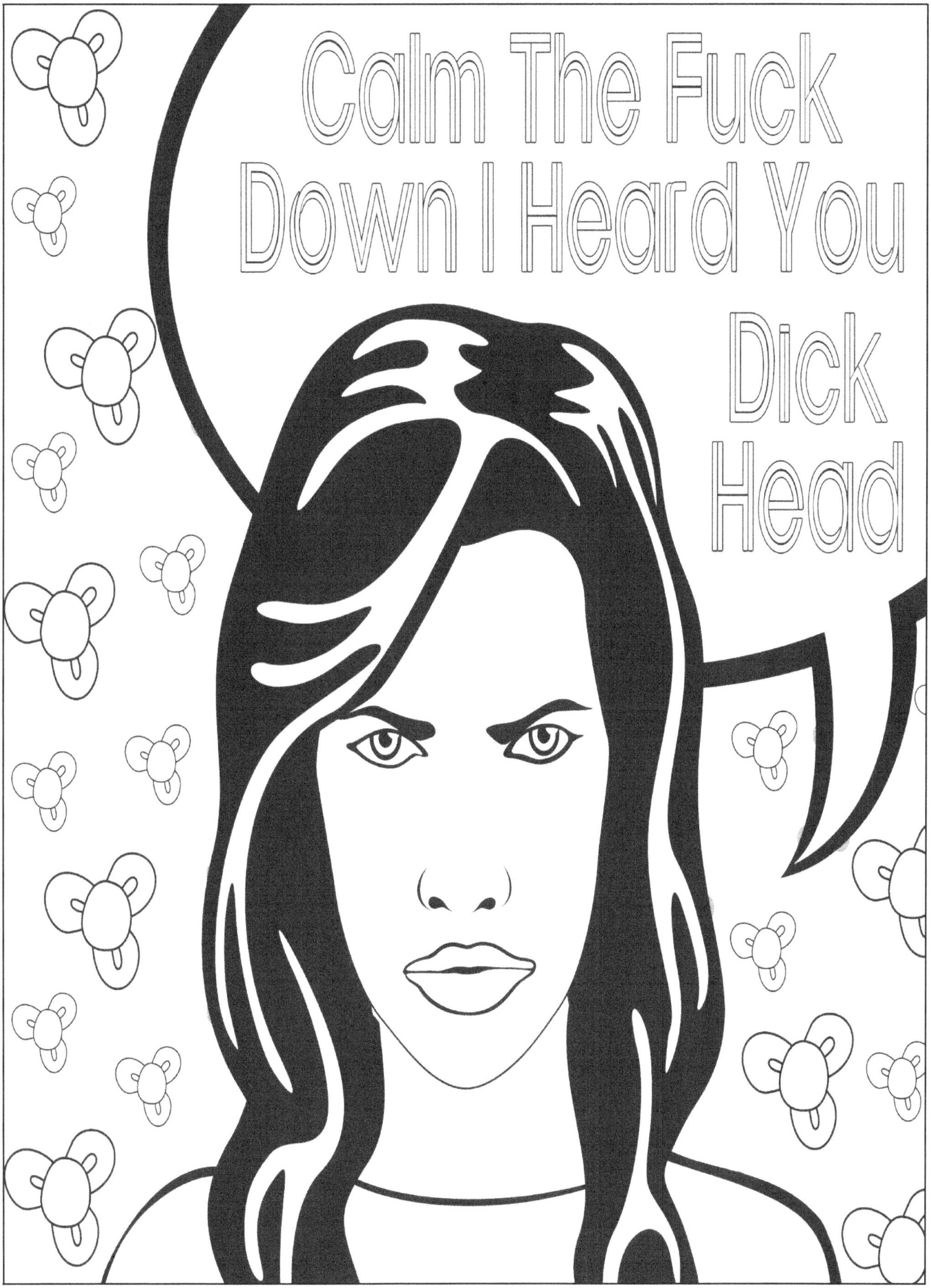
Calm The Fuck Down I Heard You Dick Head

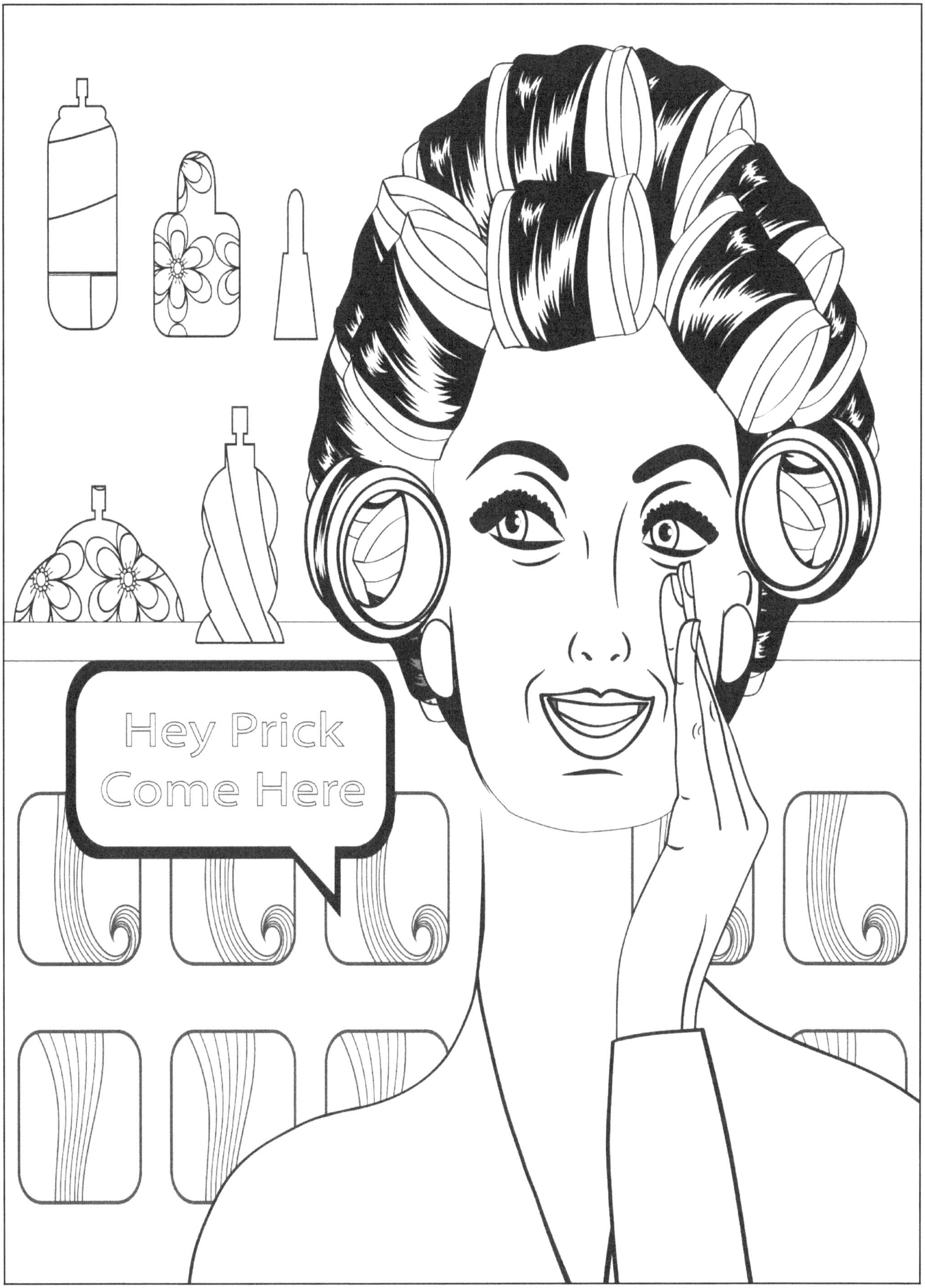
Hey Prick
Come Here

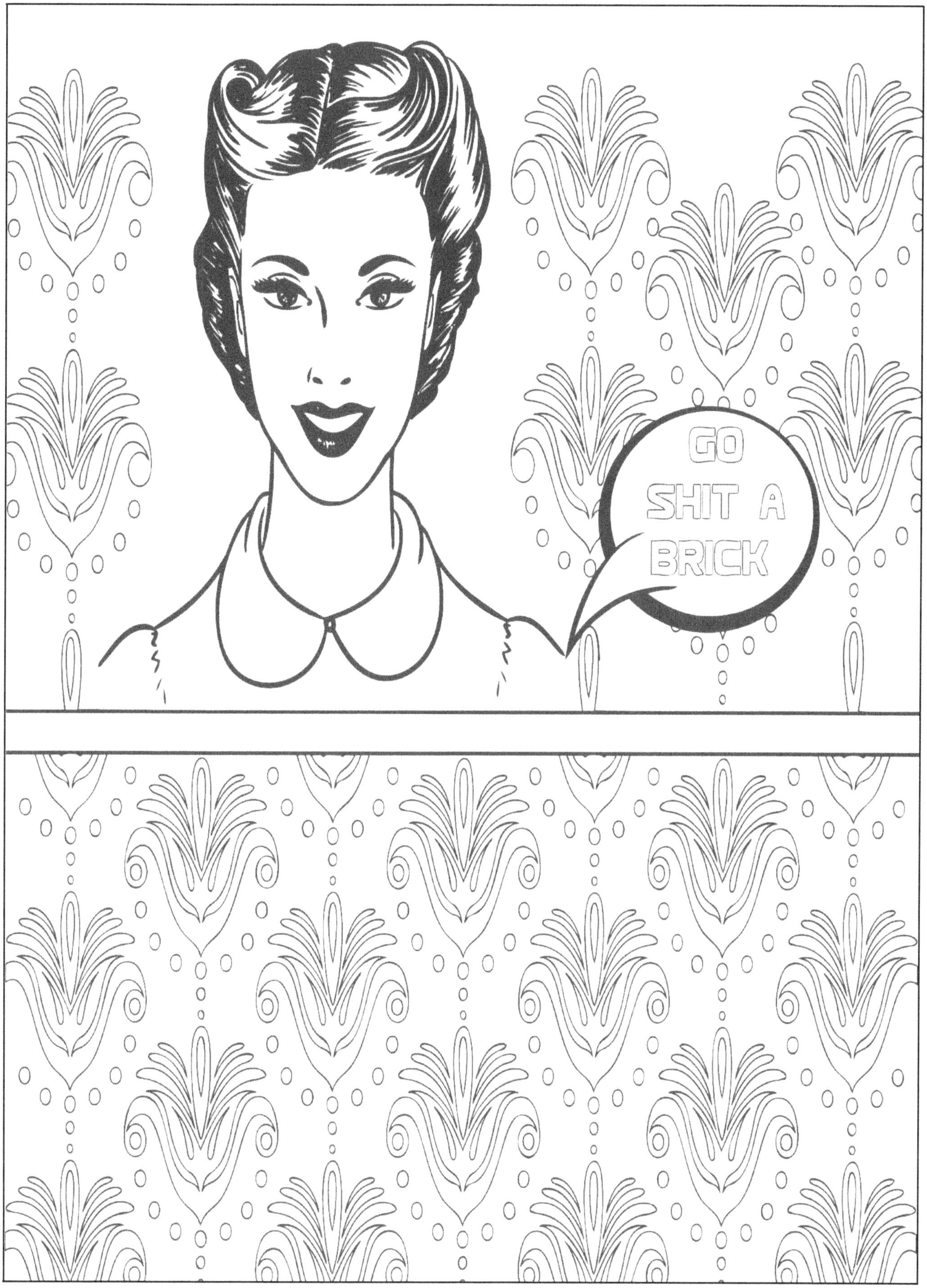
GO SHIT A BRICK

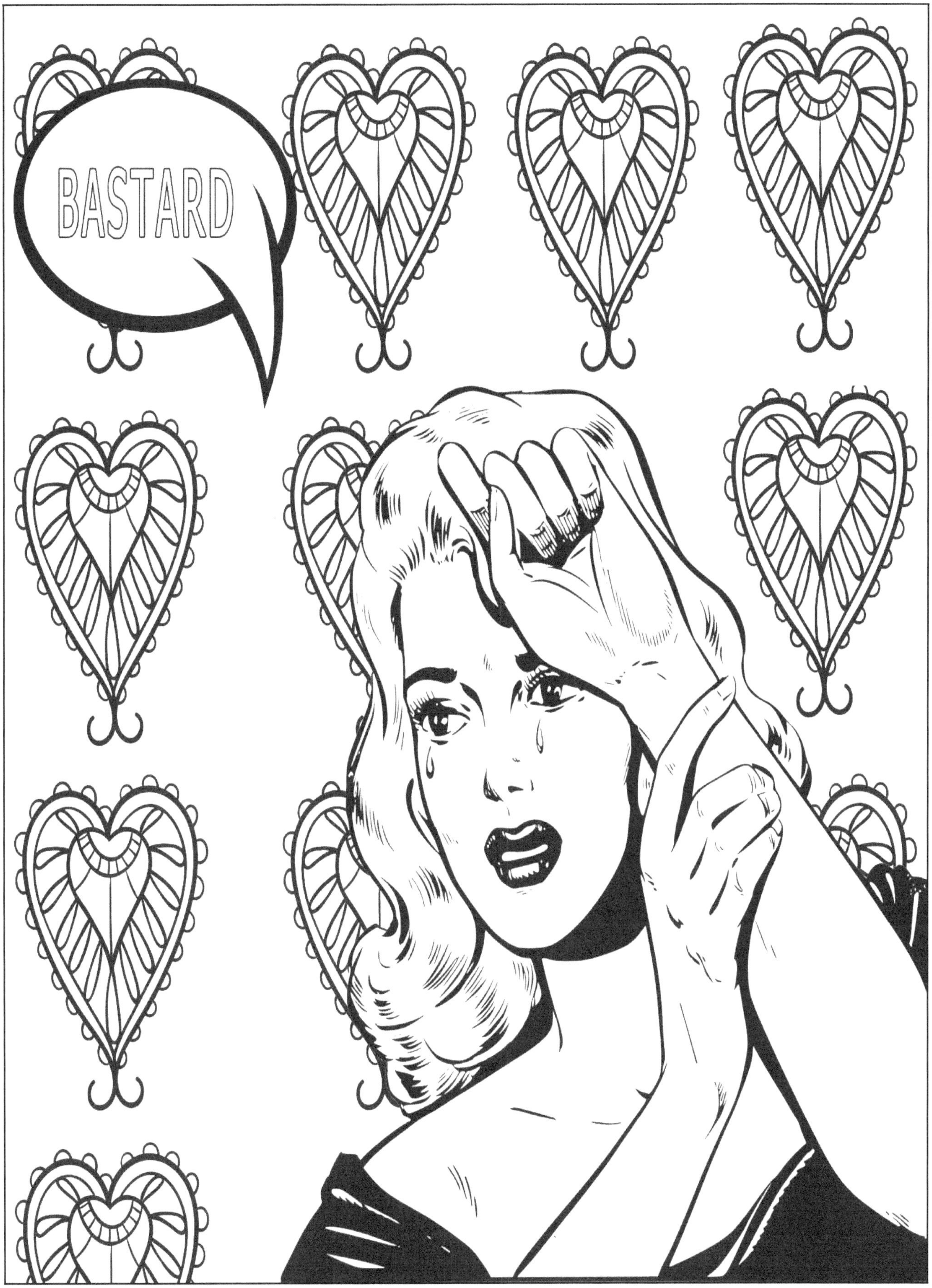
BASTARD

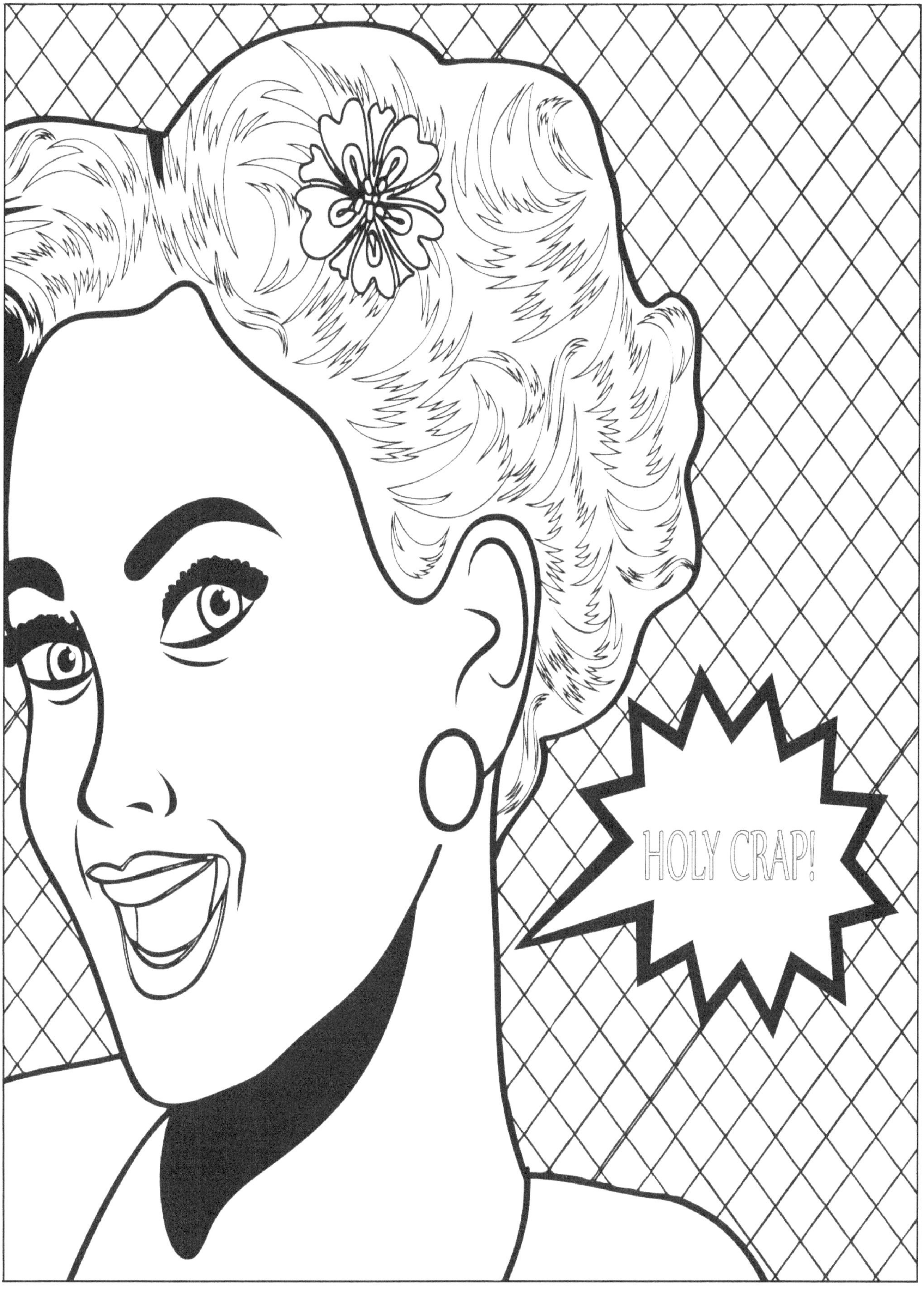
HOLY CRAP!

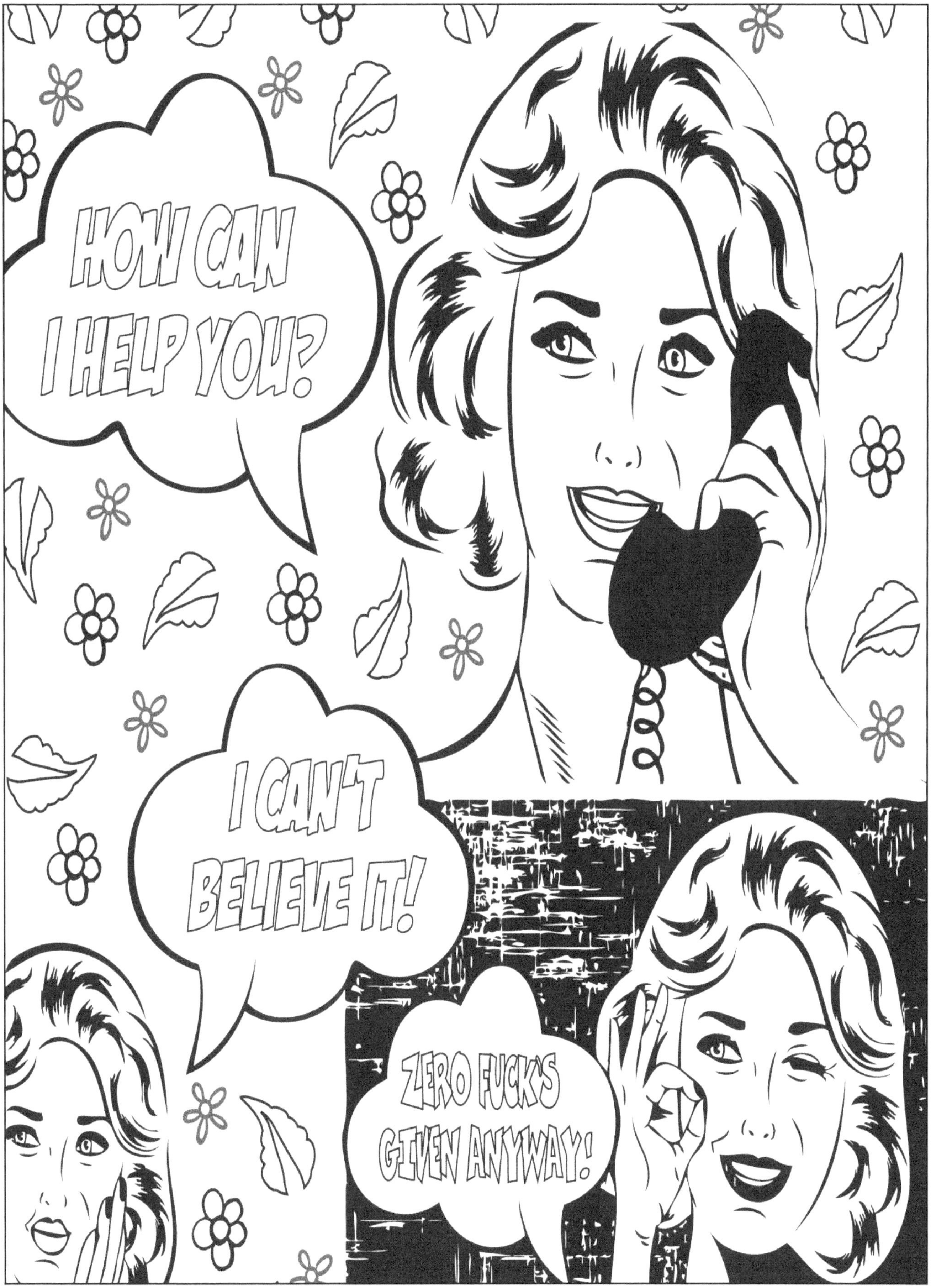
HOW CAN I HELP YOU?
I CAN'T BELIEVE IT!
ZERO FUCK'S GIVEN ANYWAY!

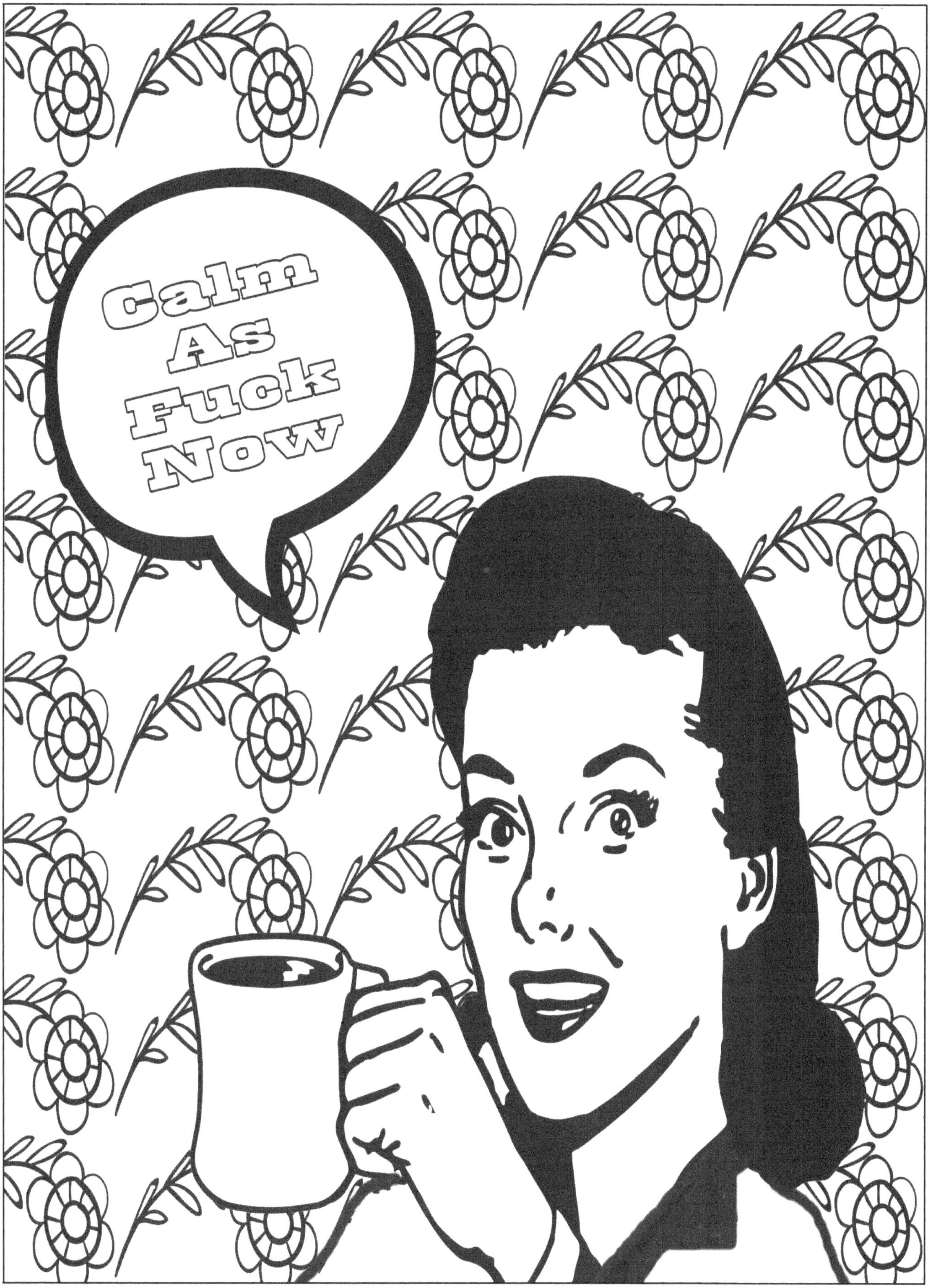
Calm
As
Fuck
Now

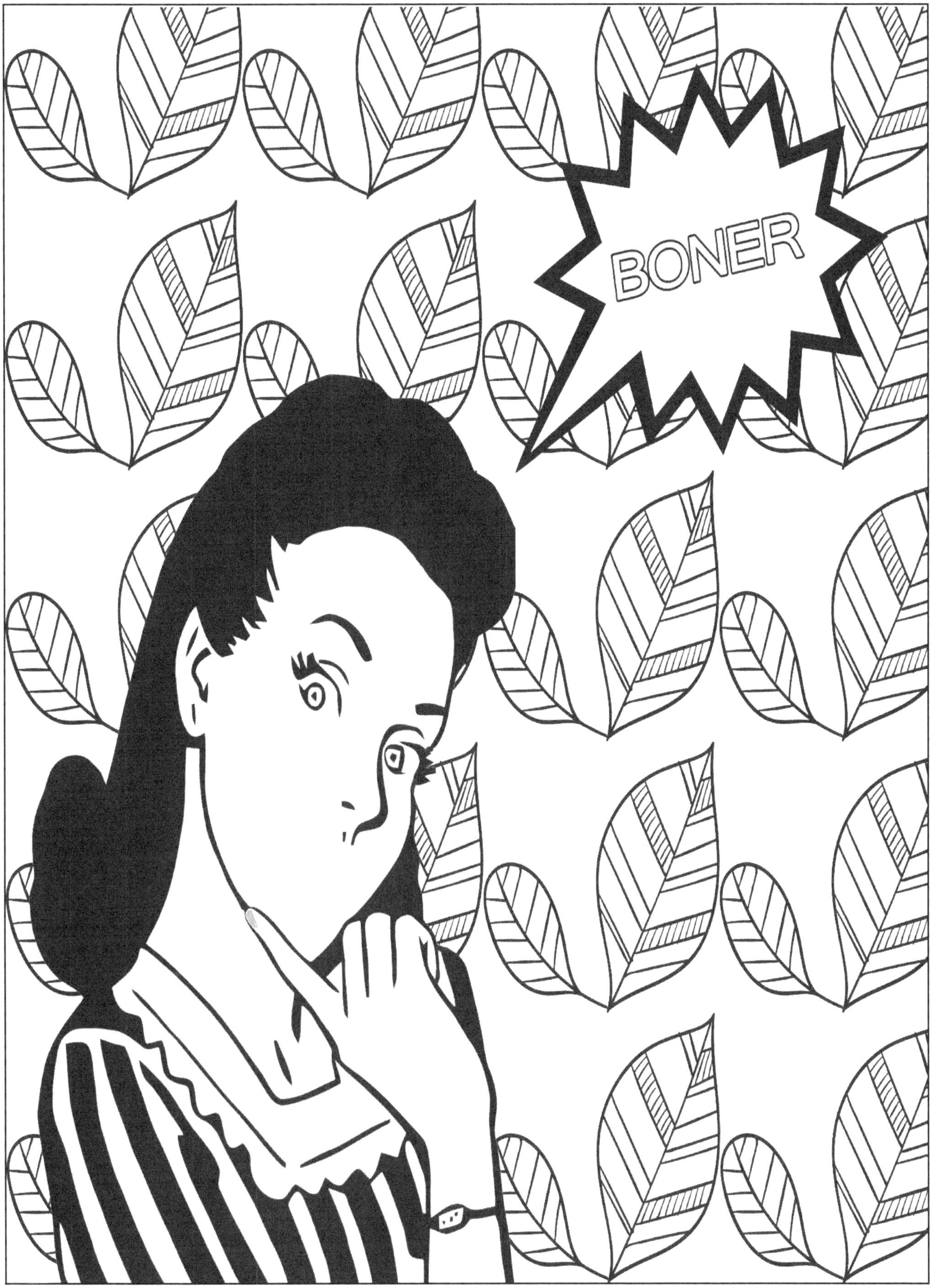
BONER

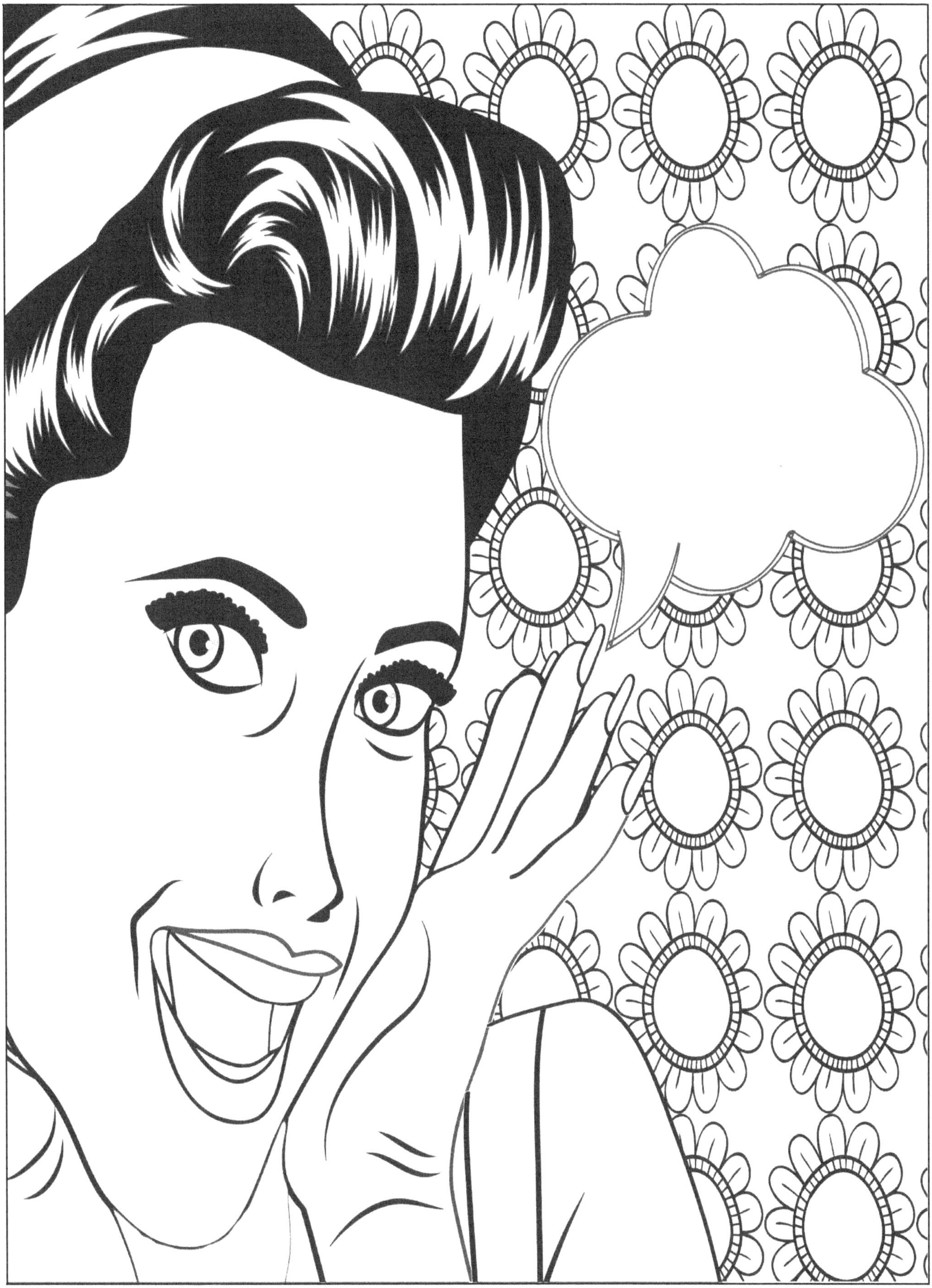

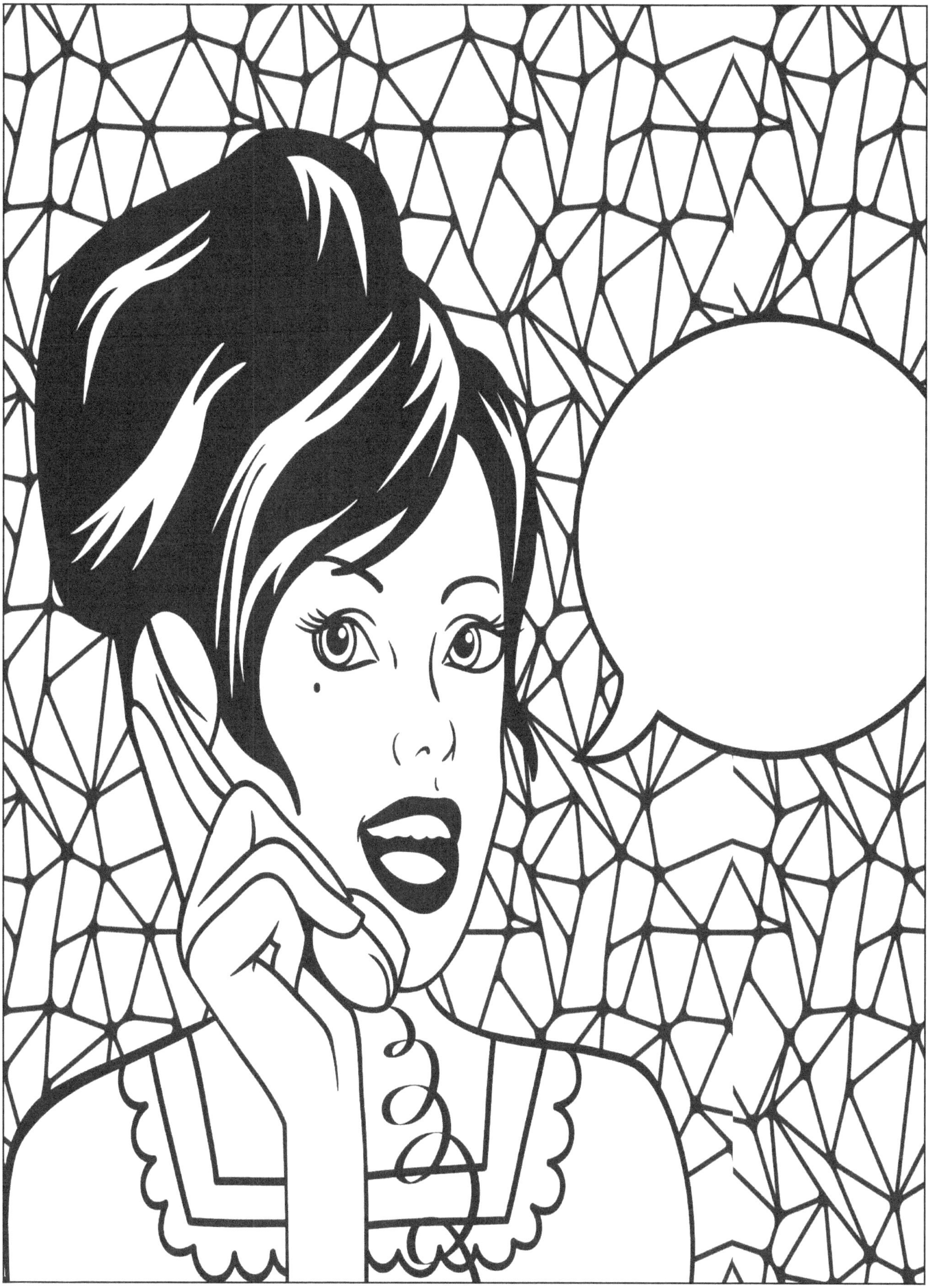

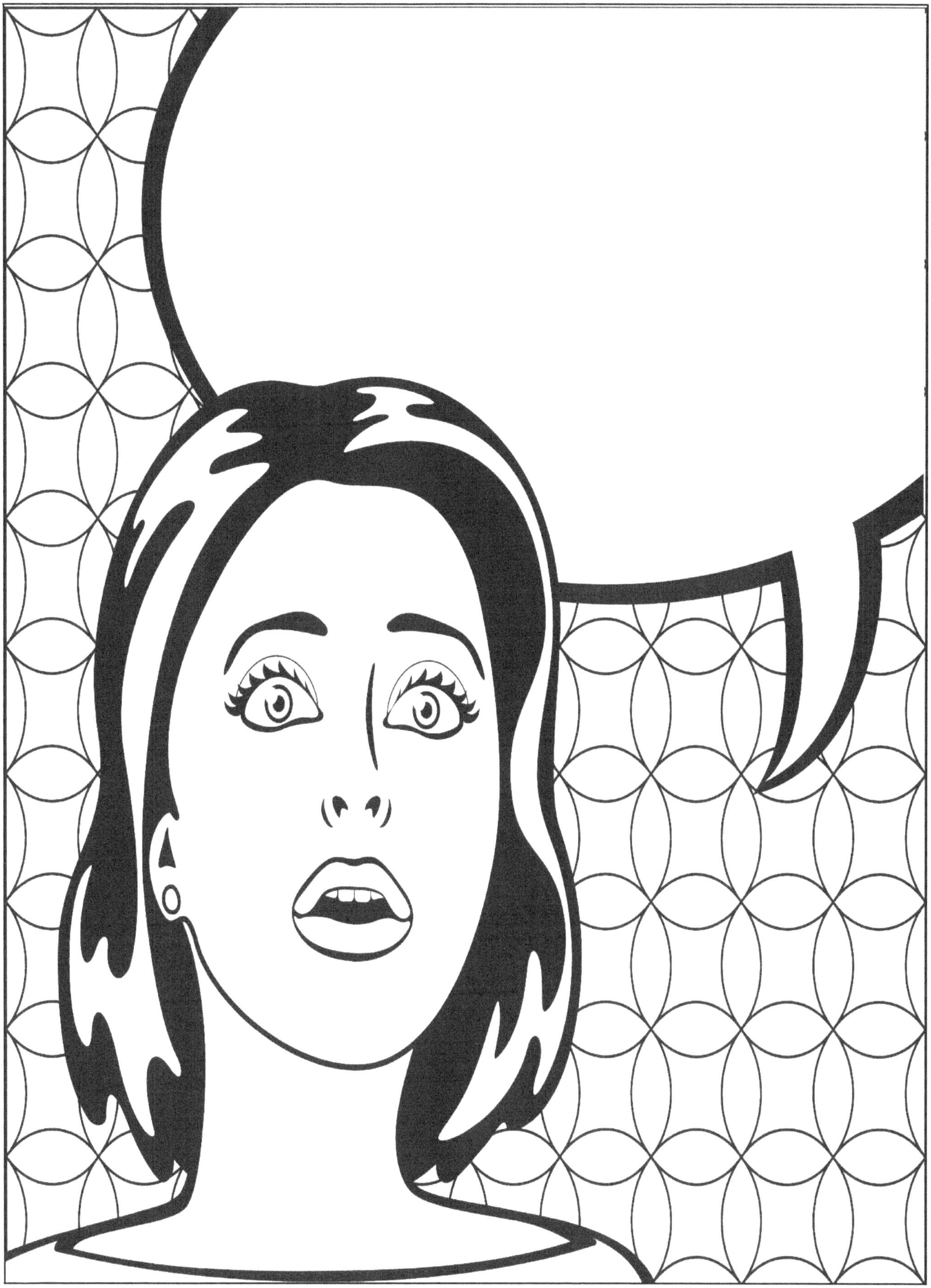

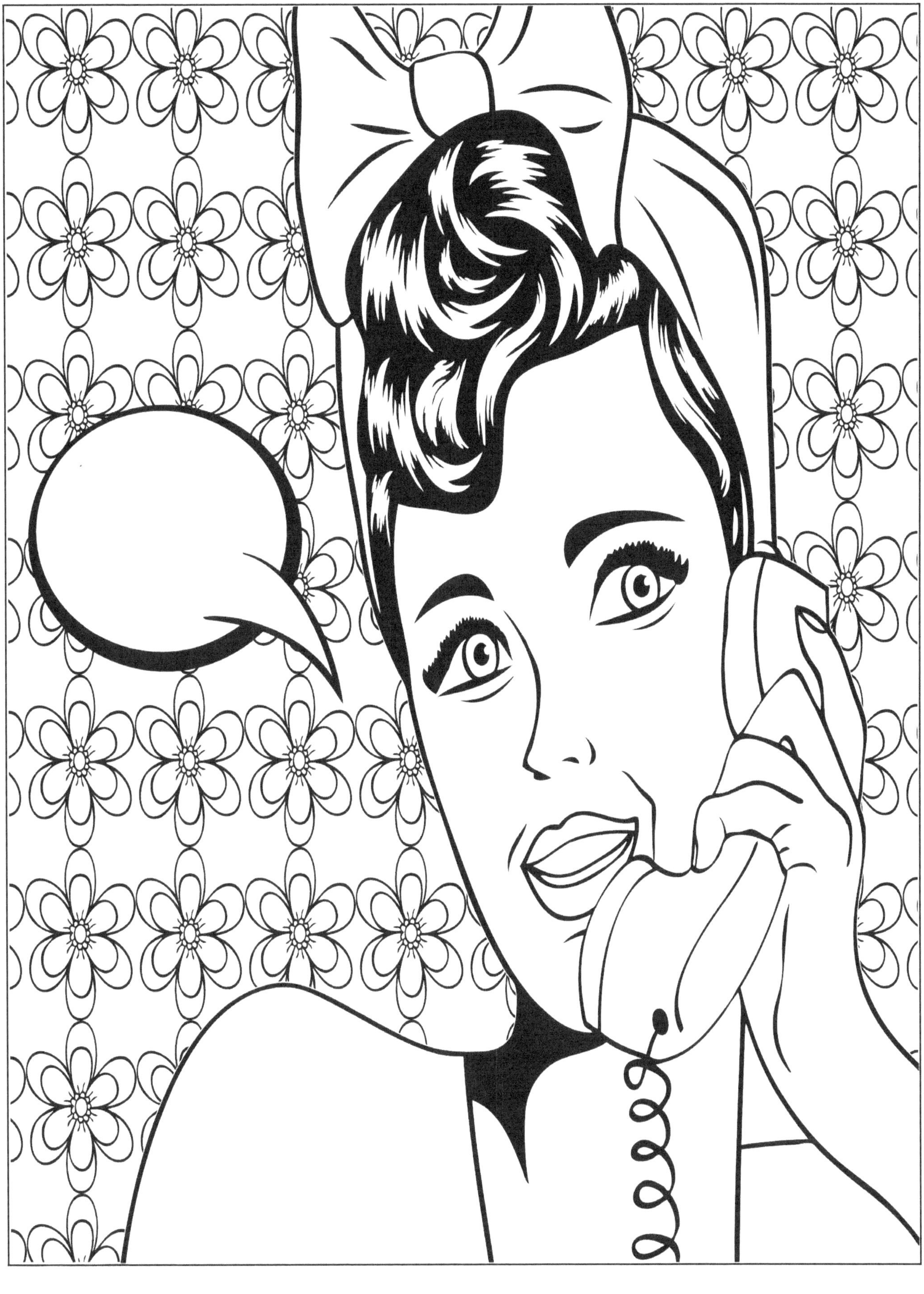

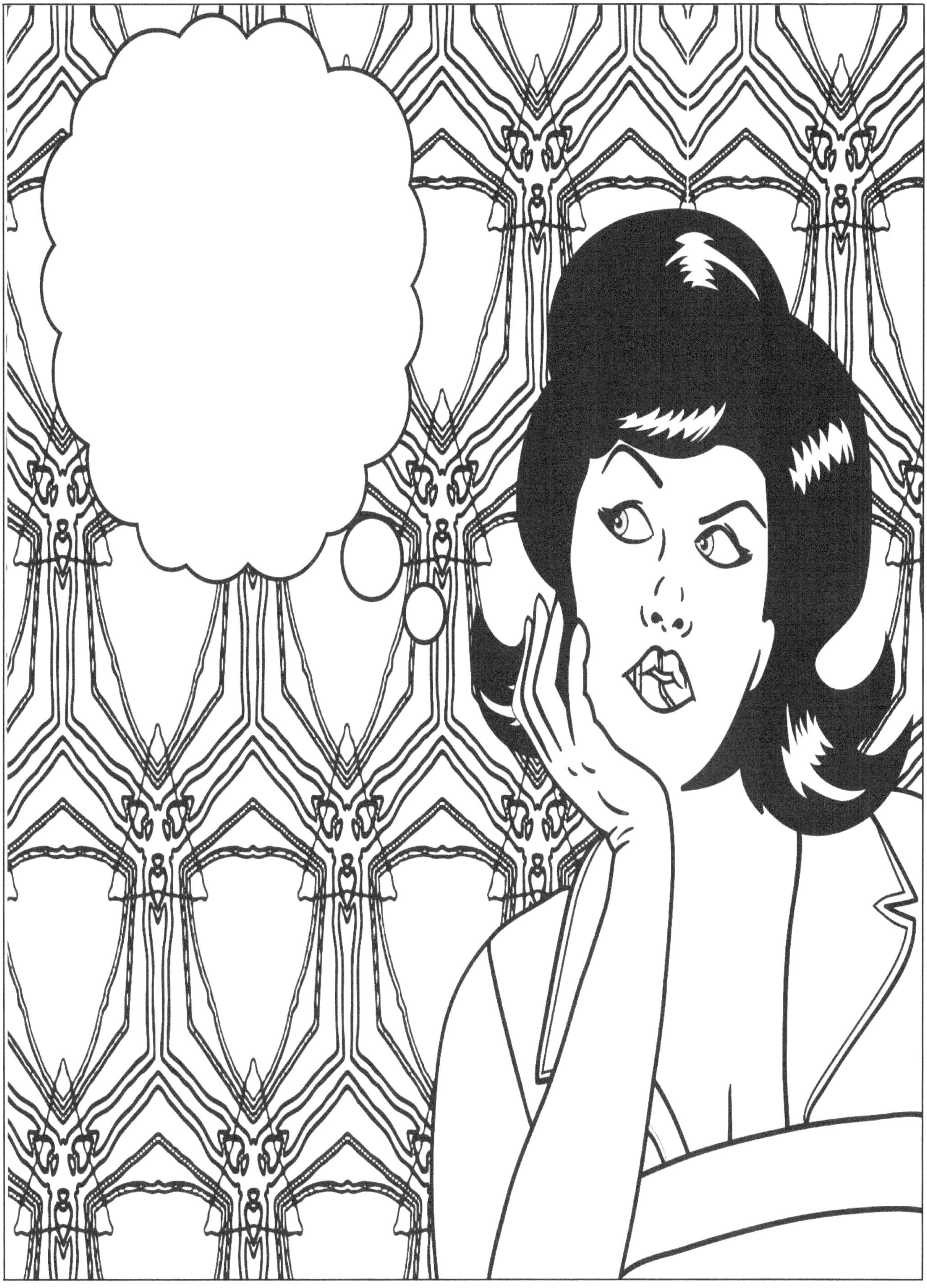

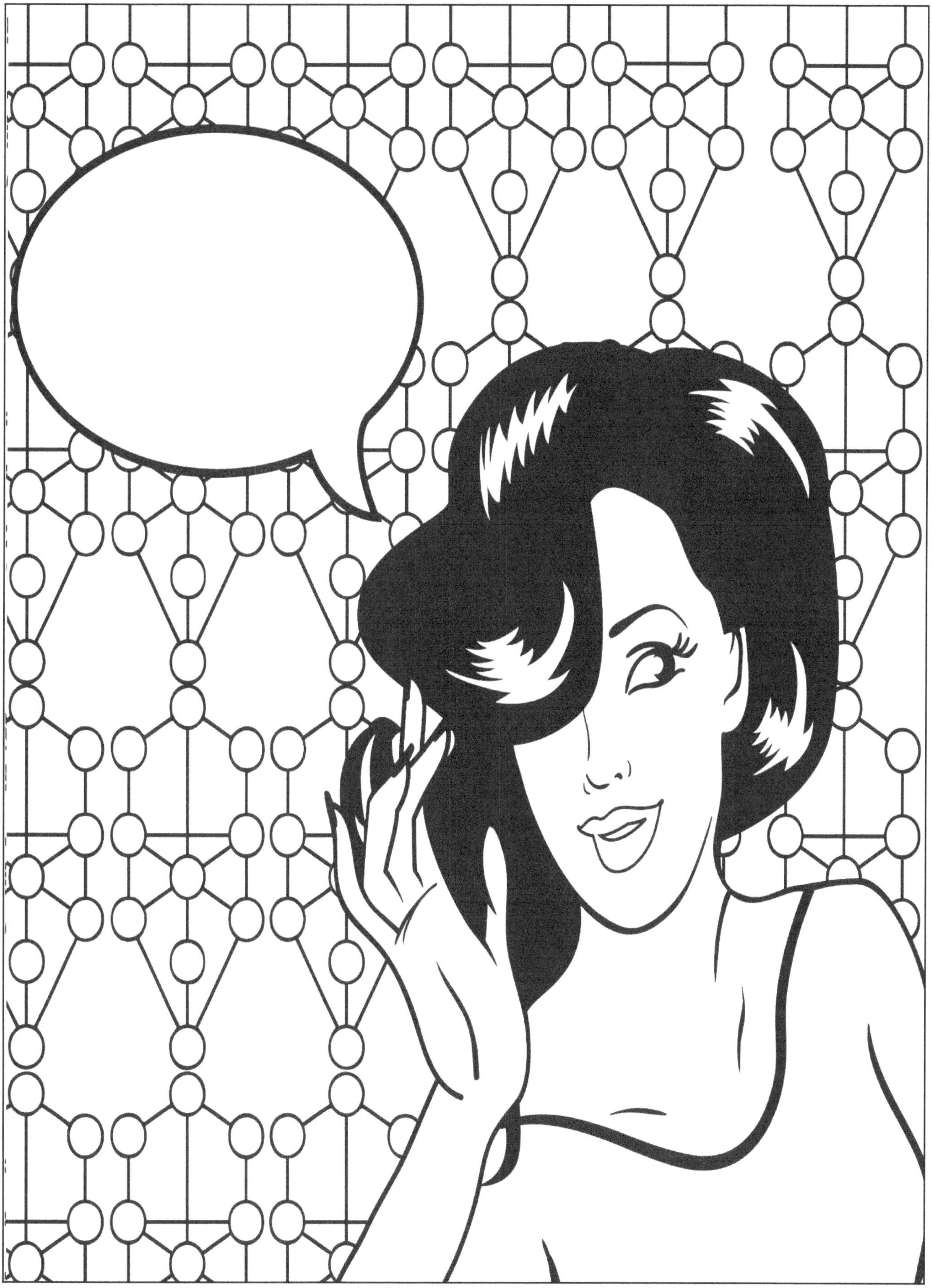

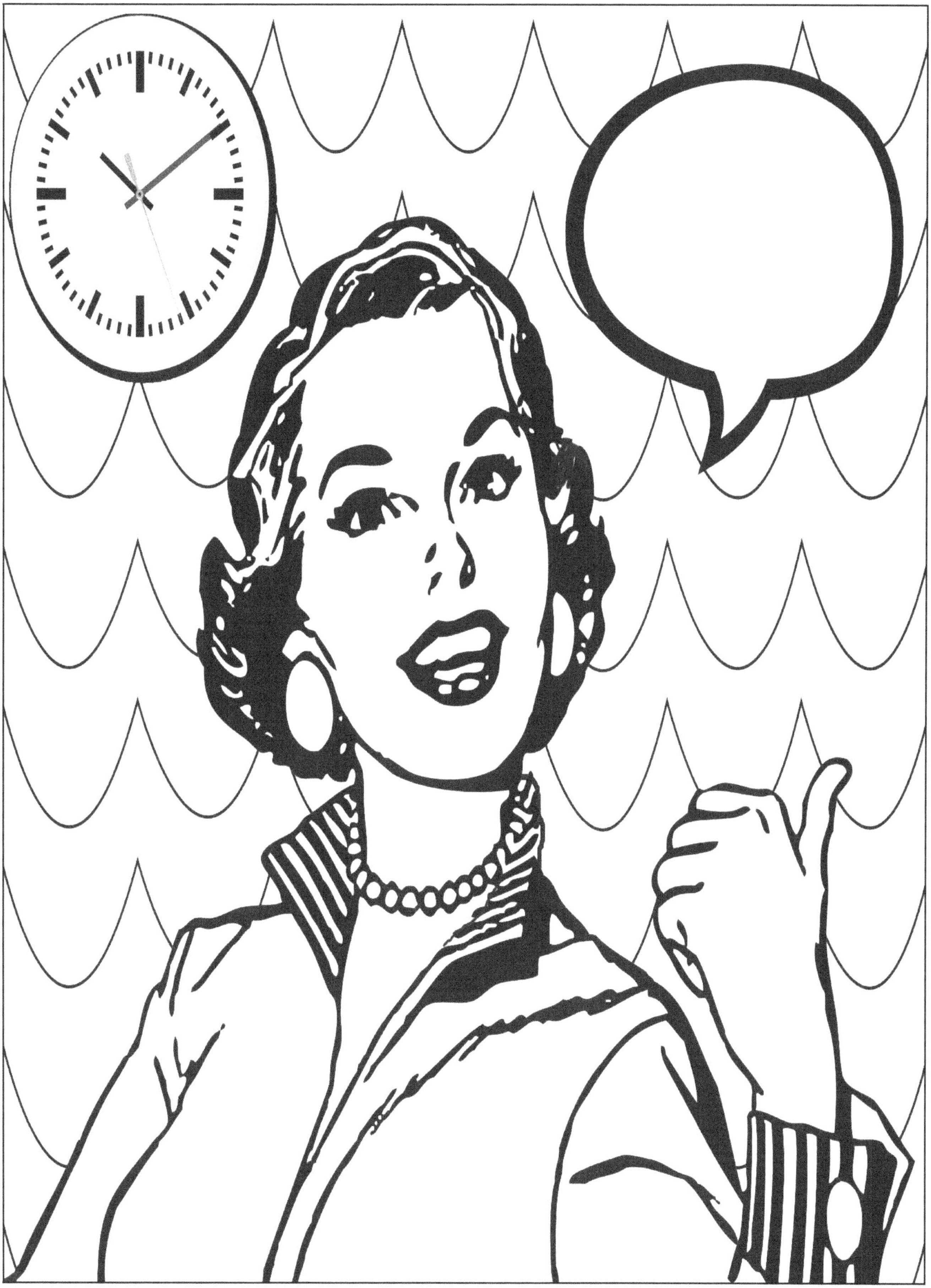

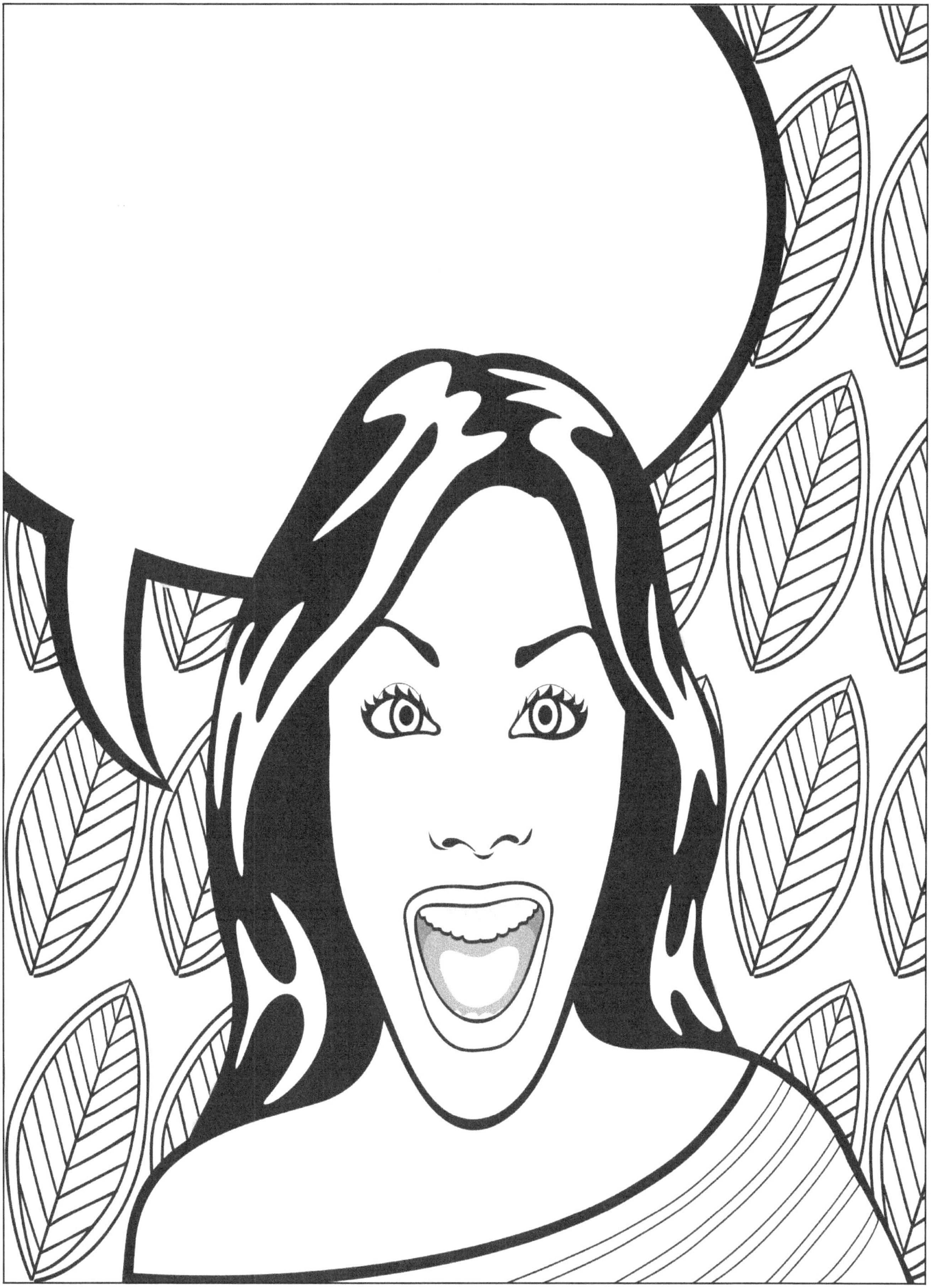

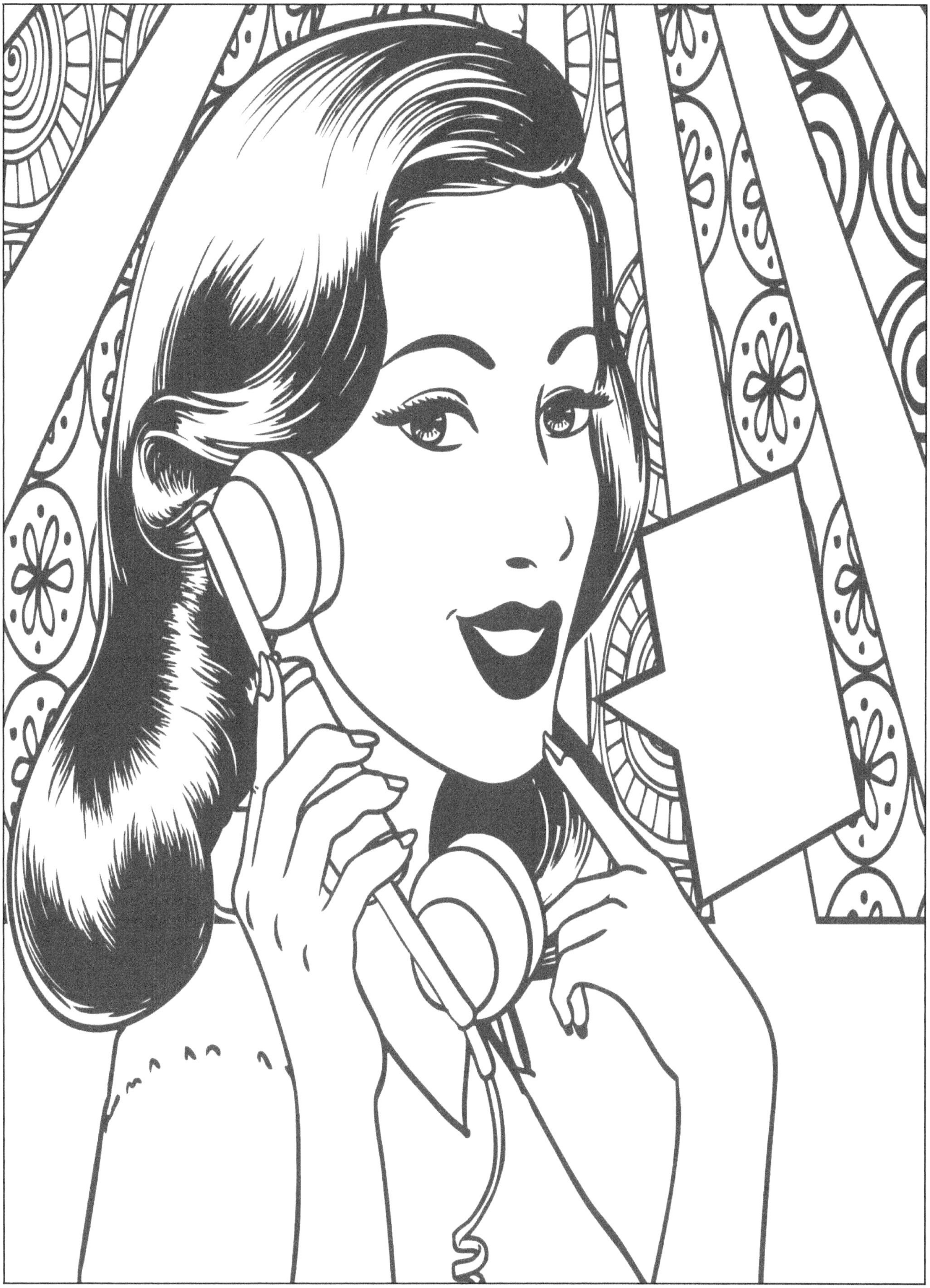

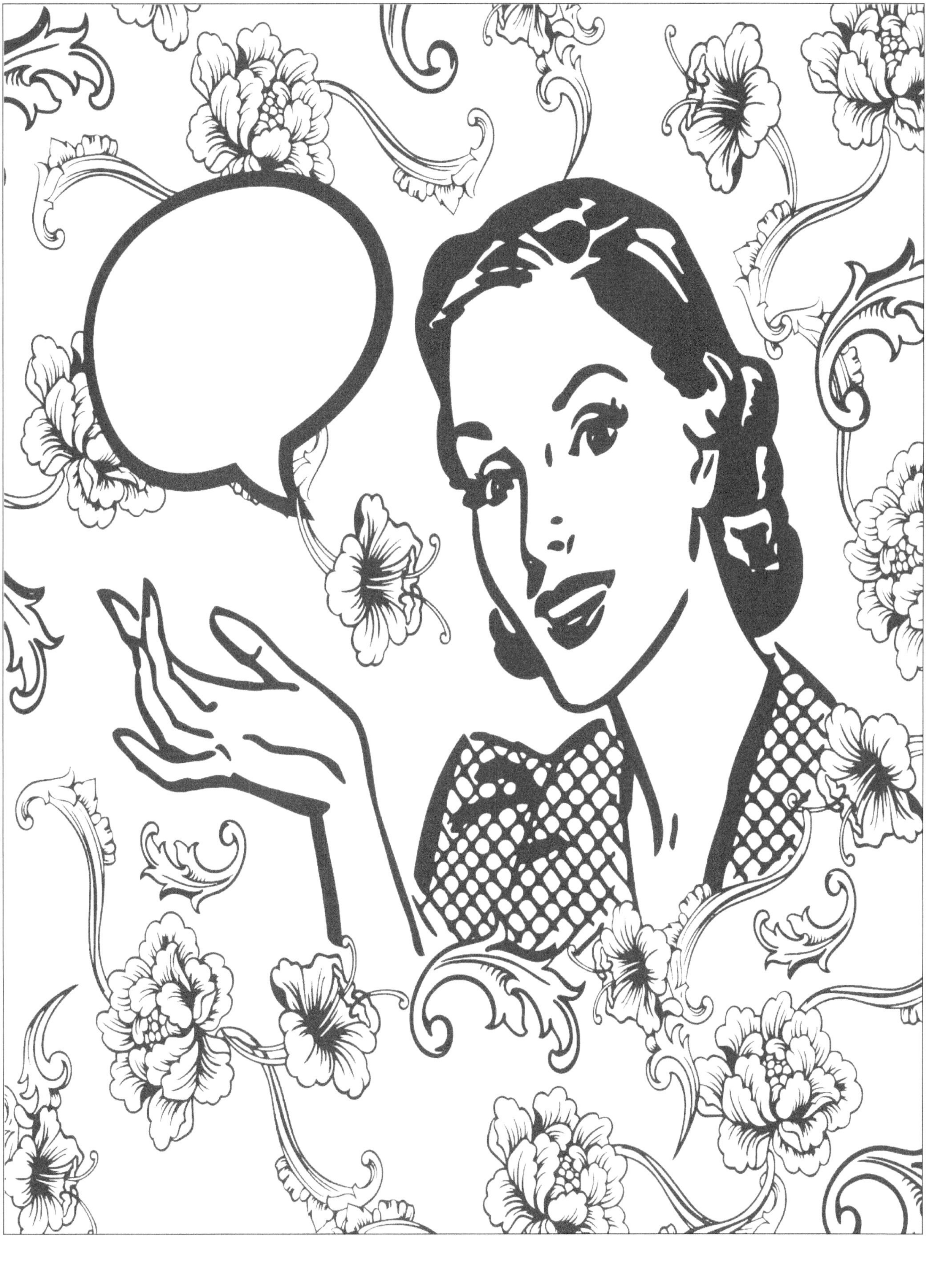

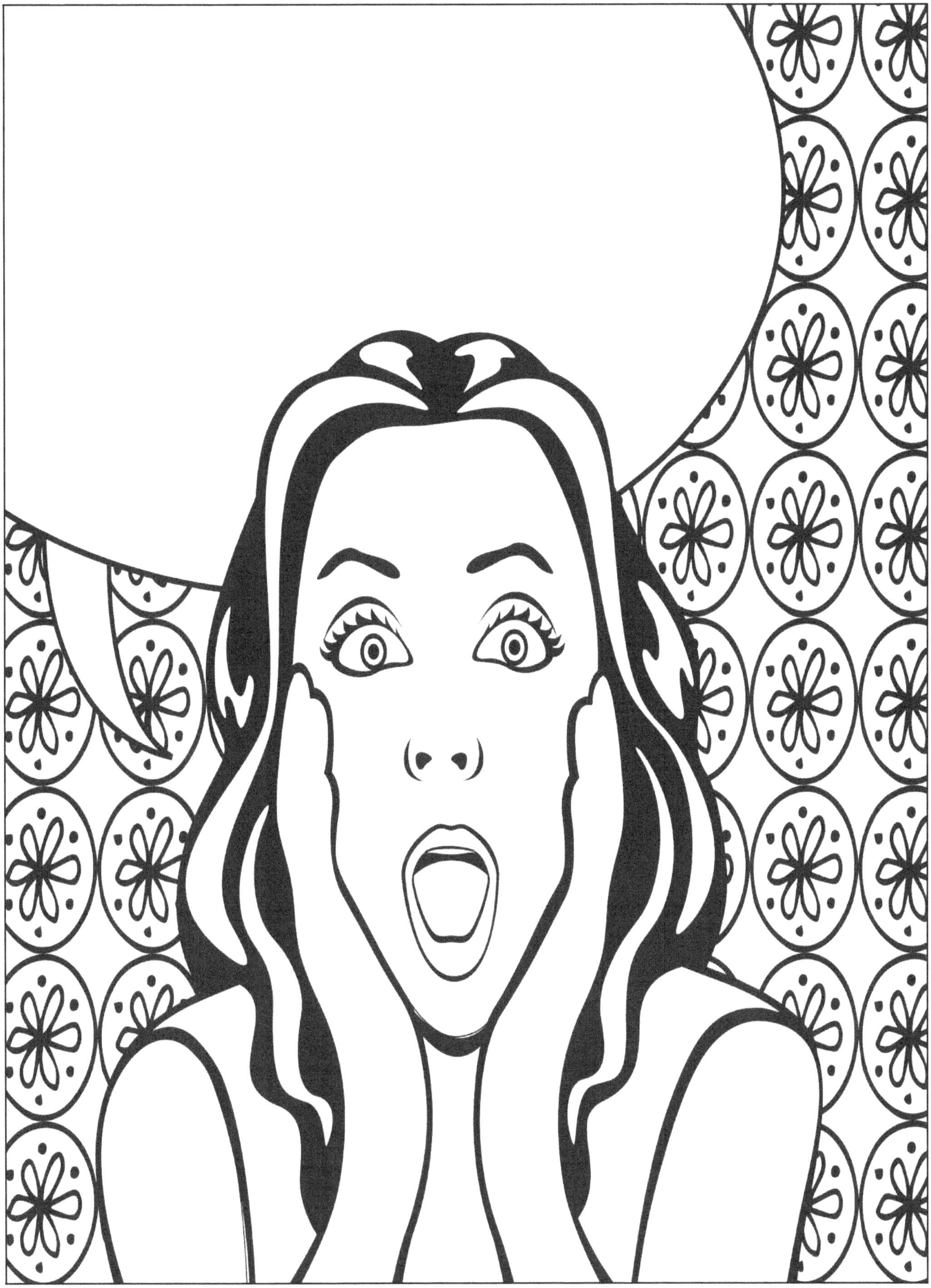

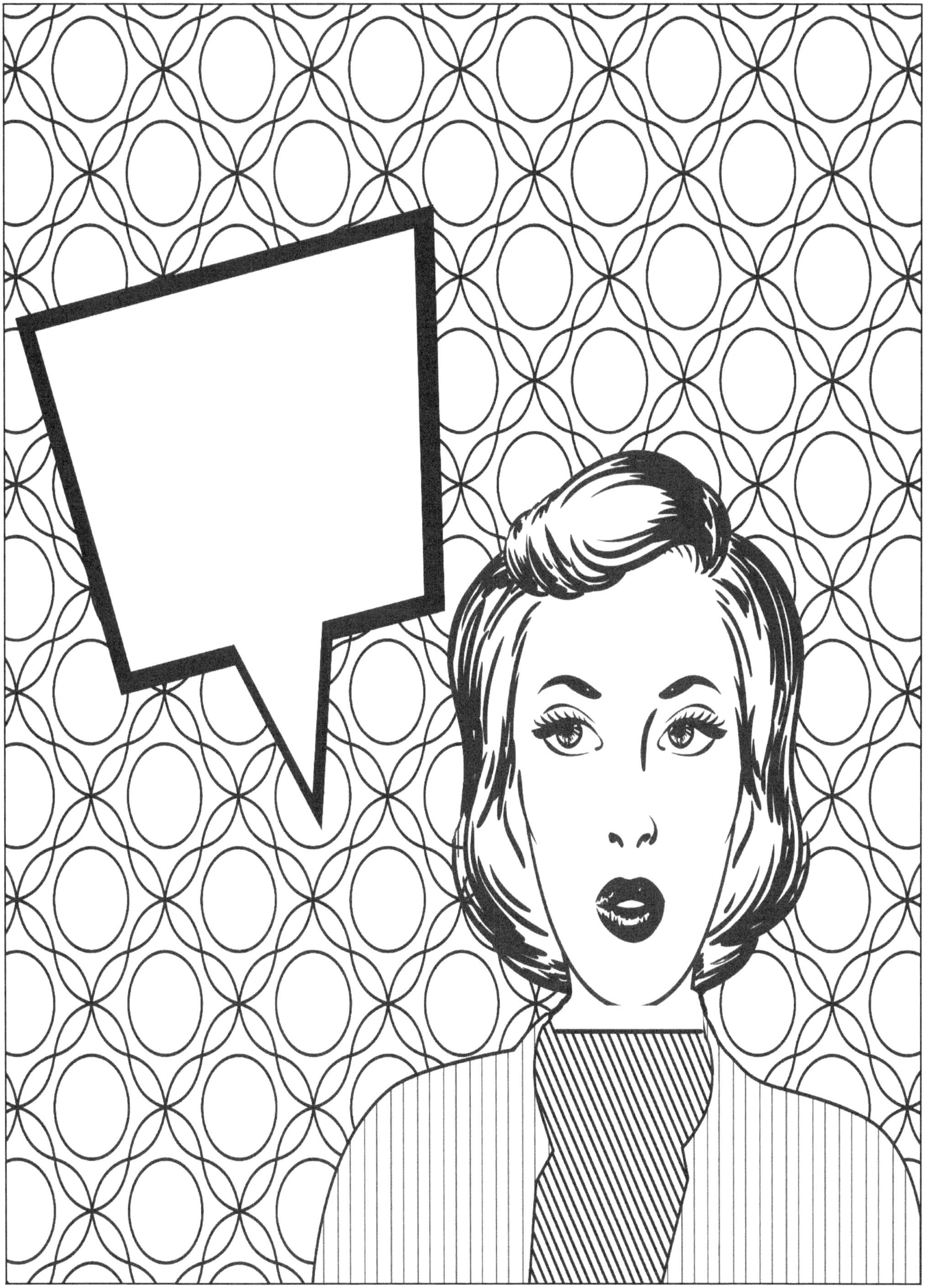

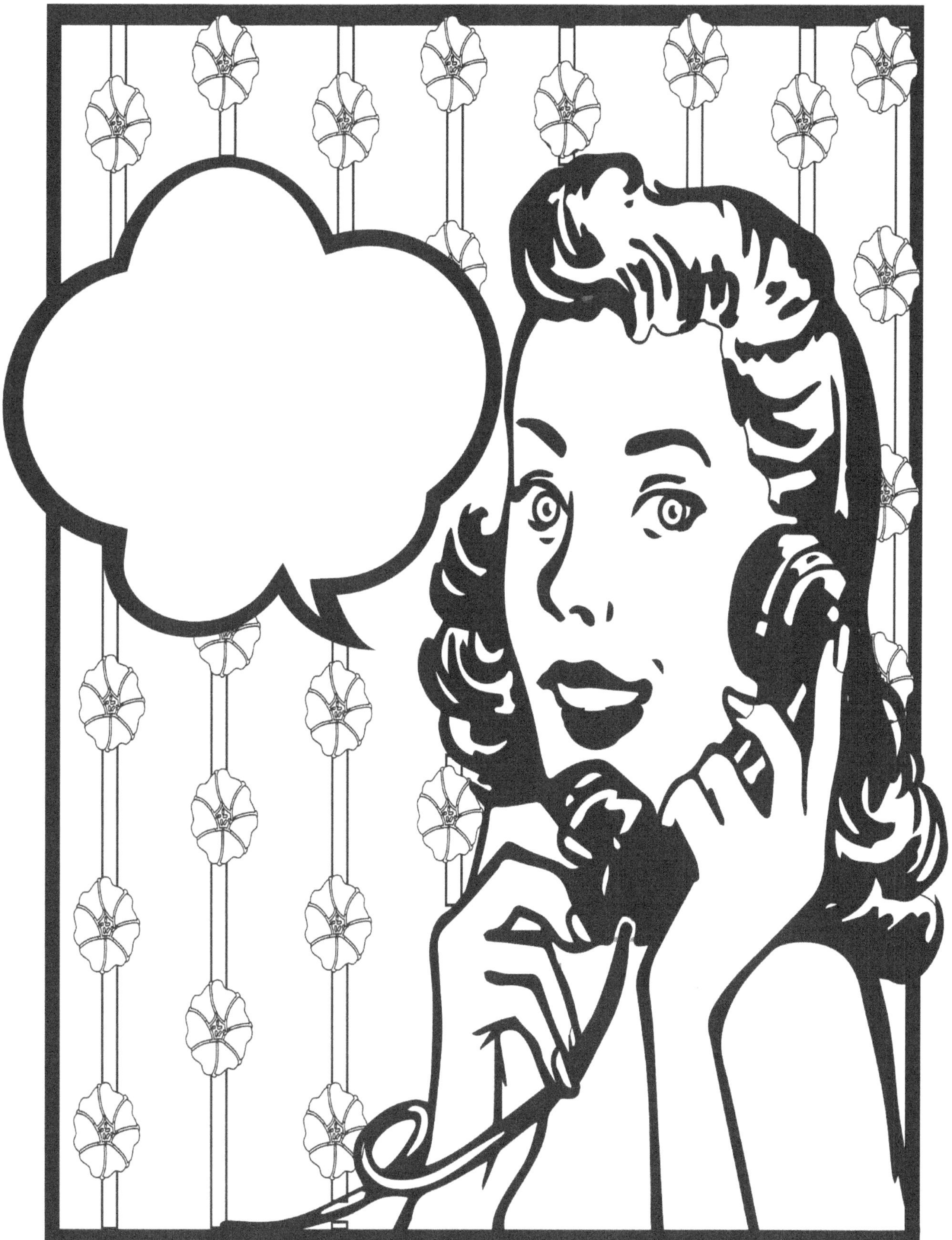

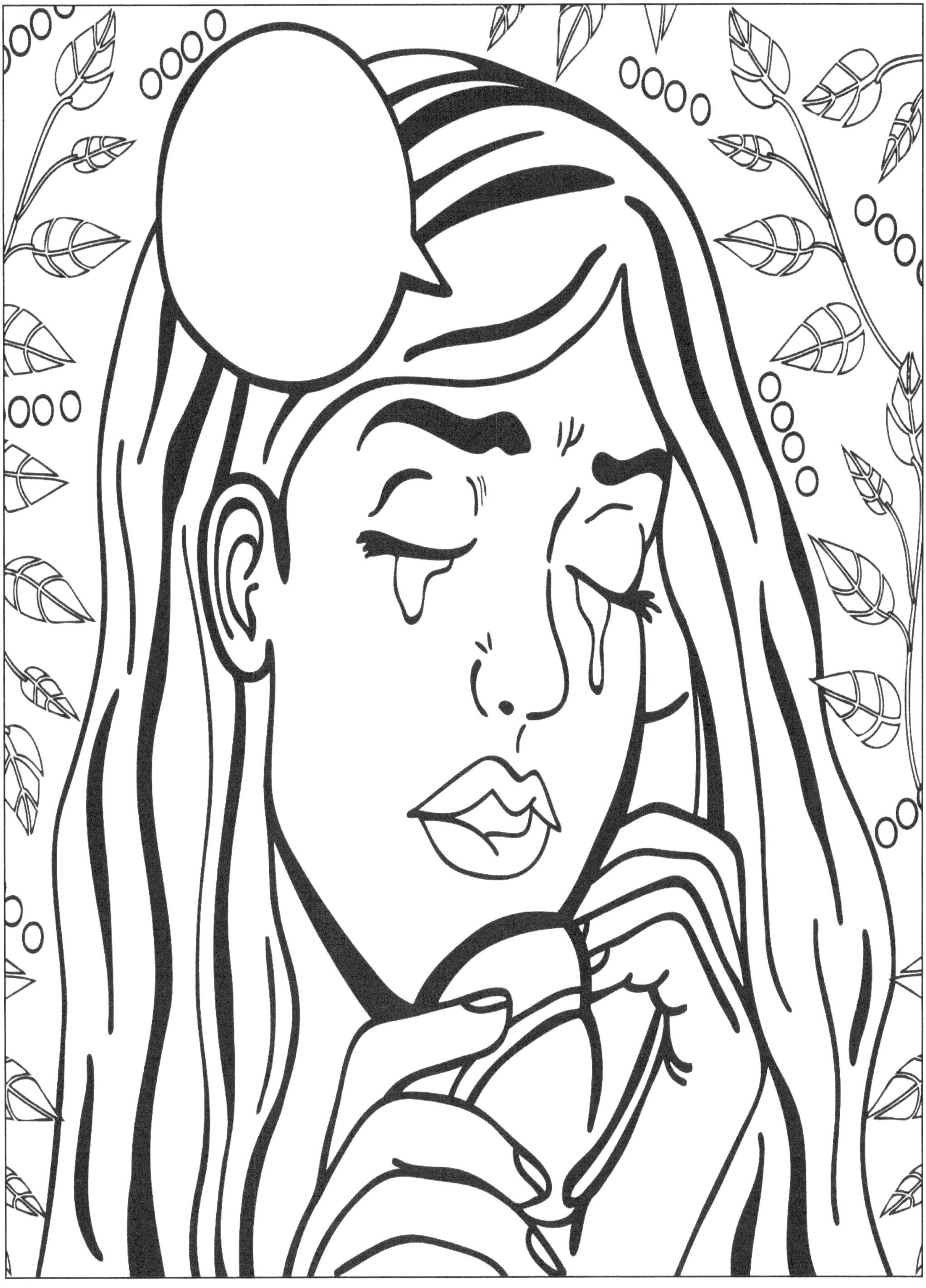

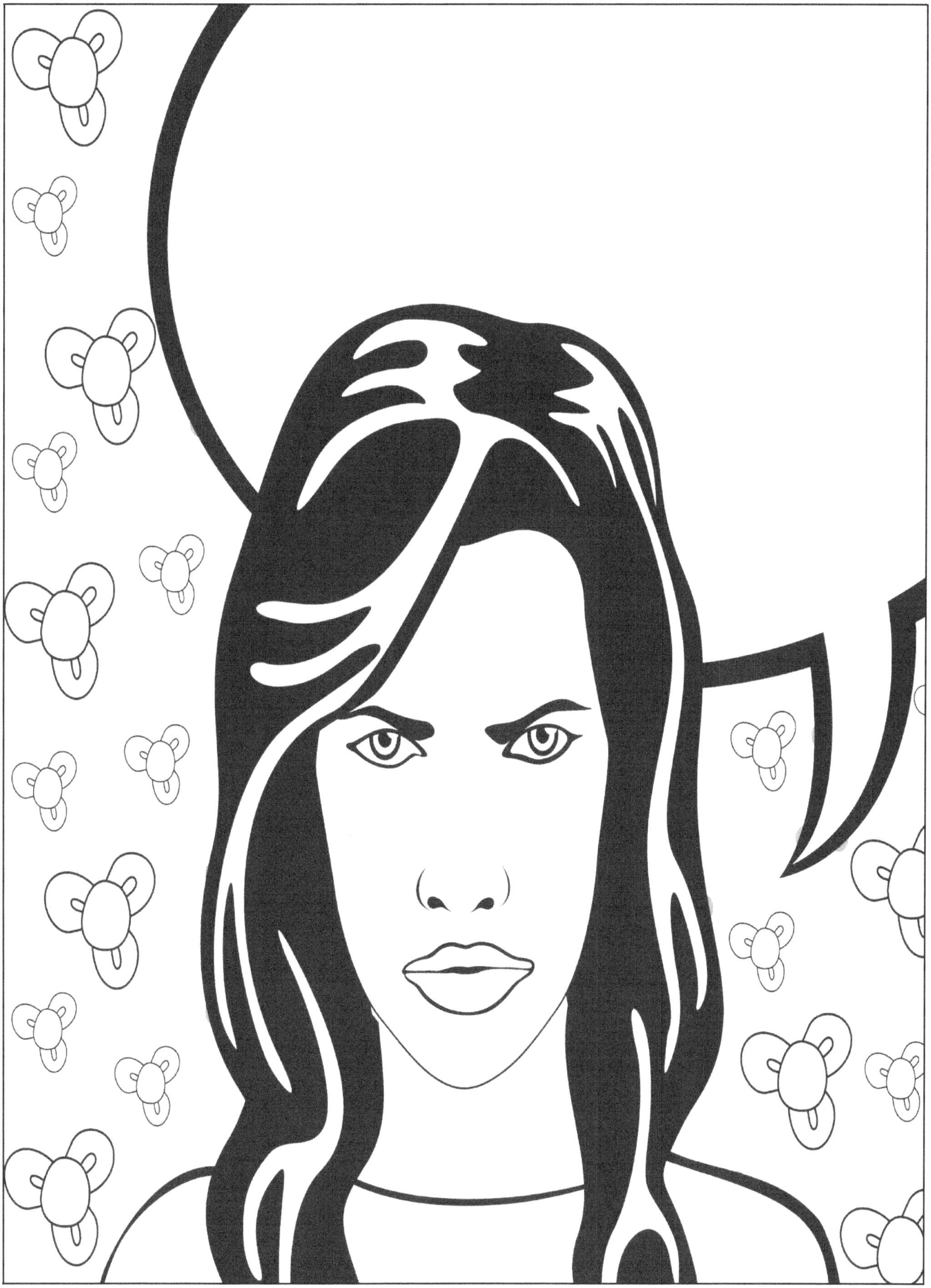

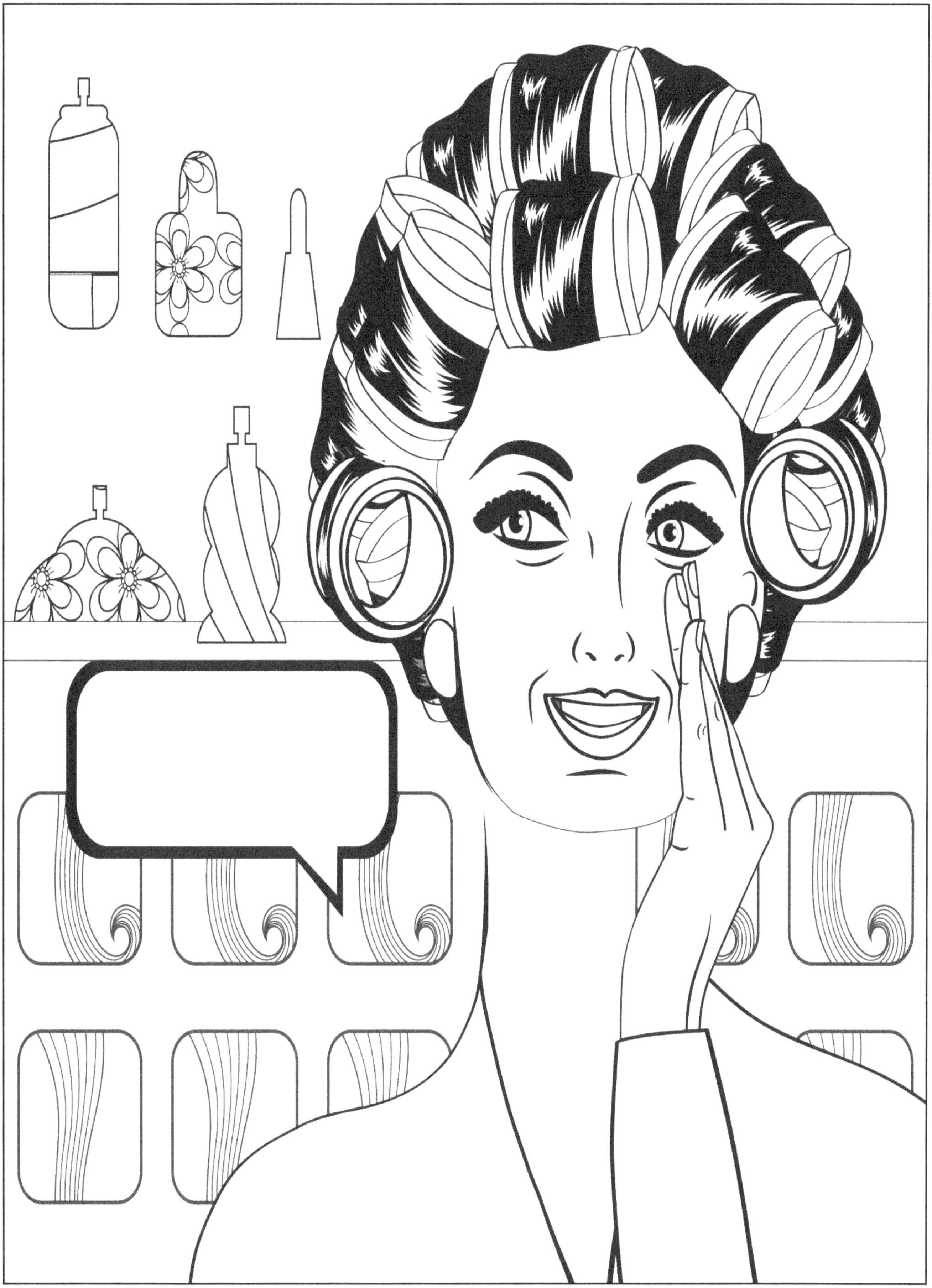

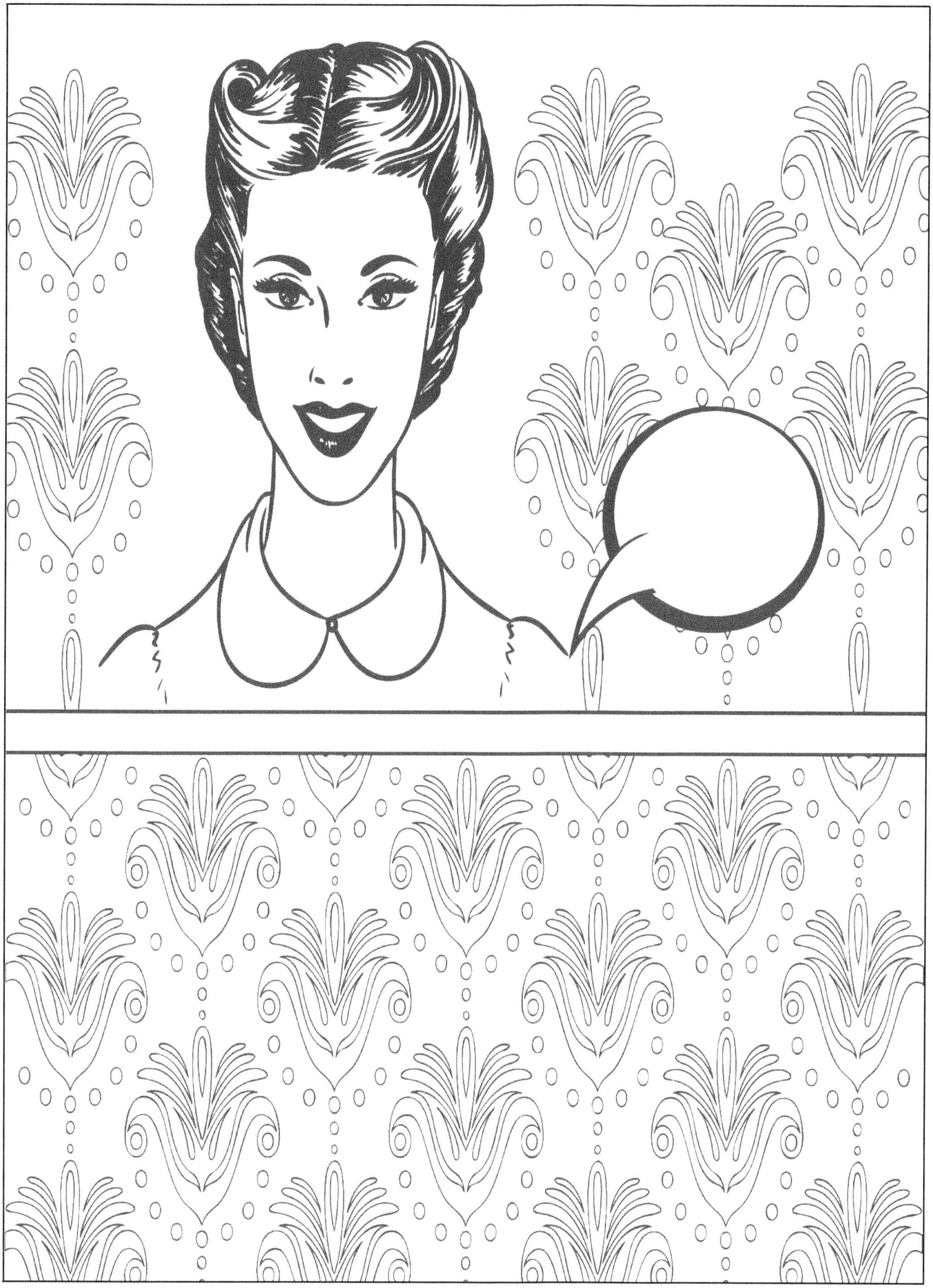

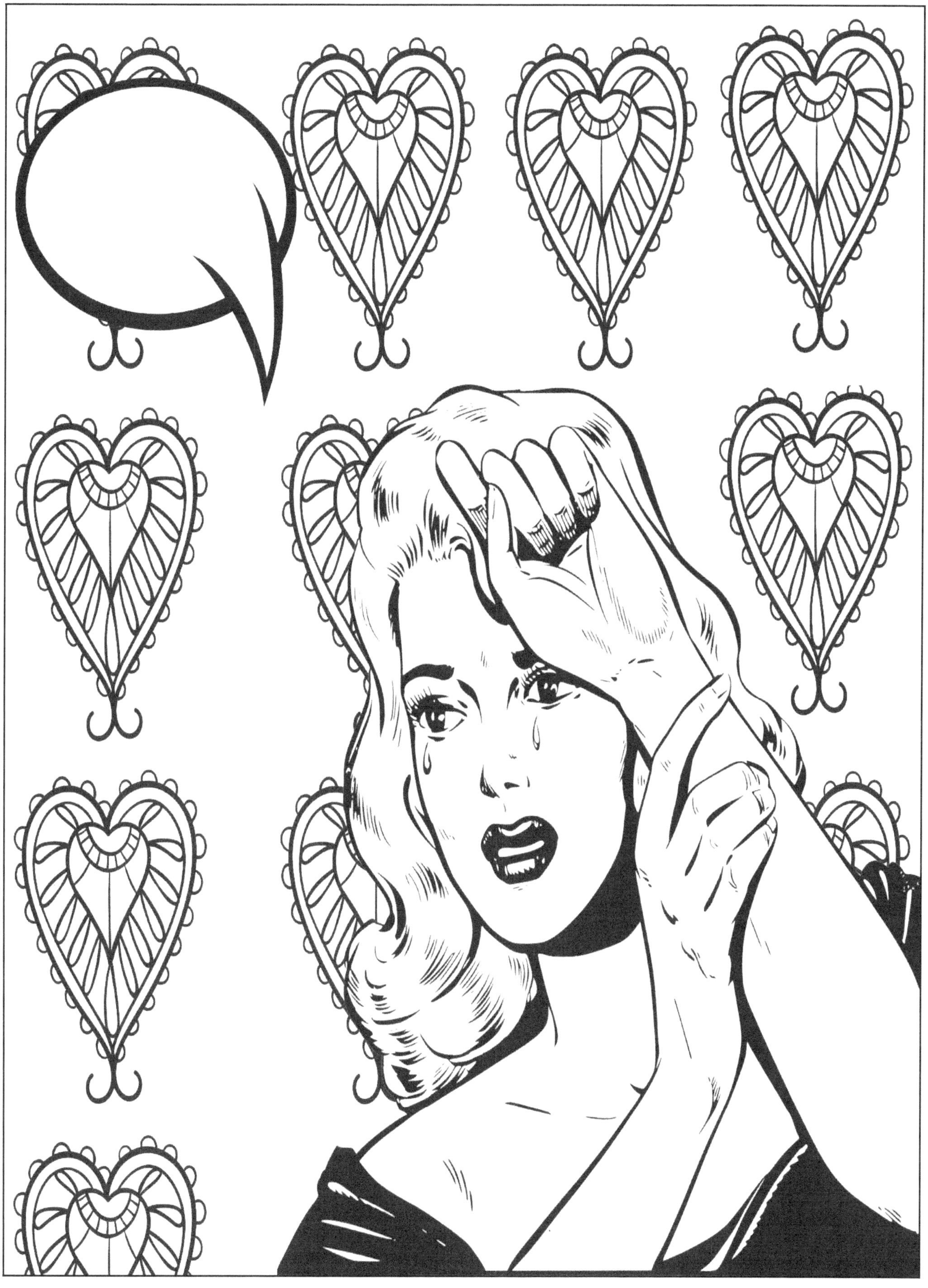

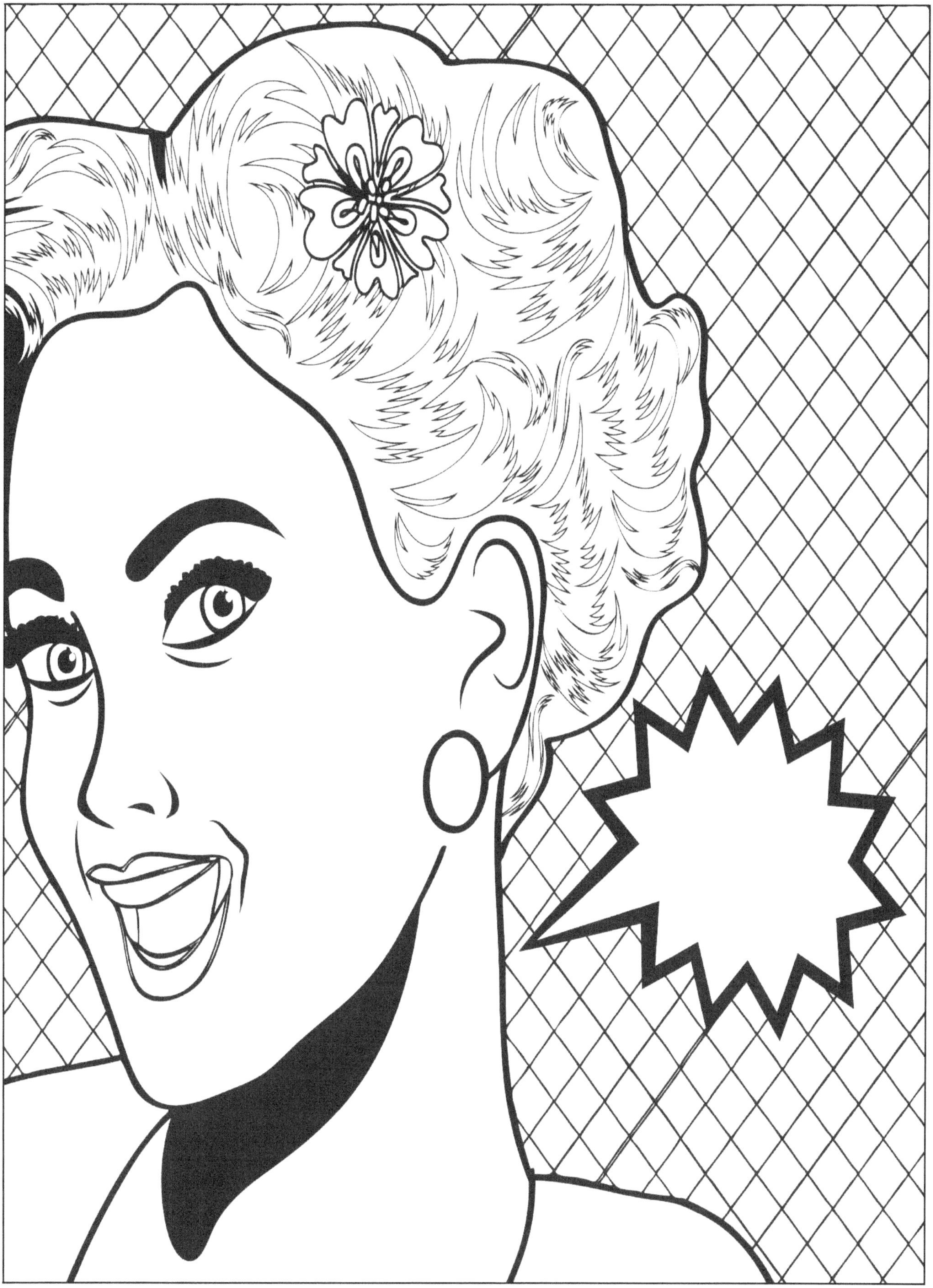

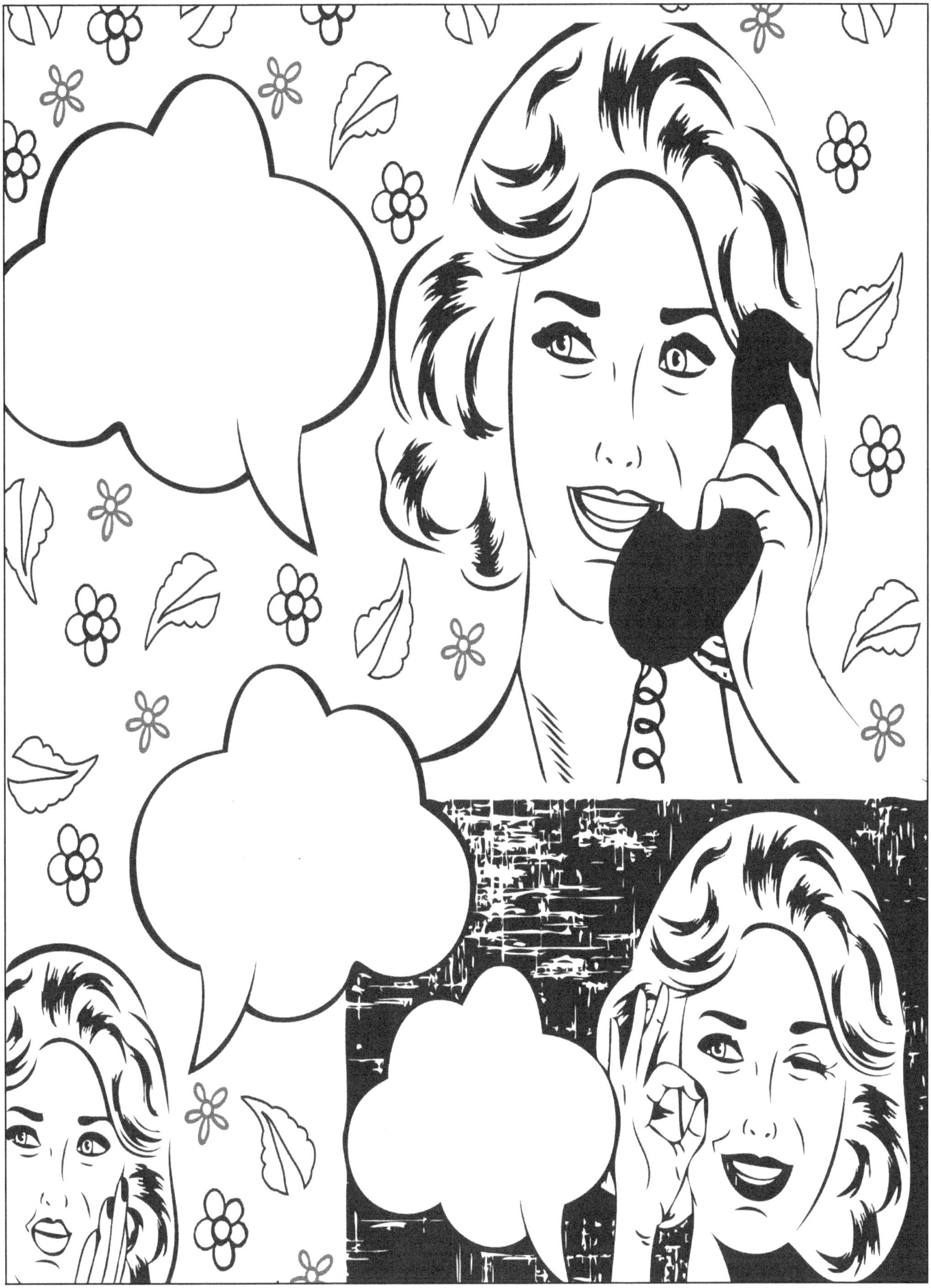

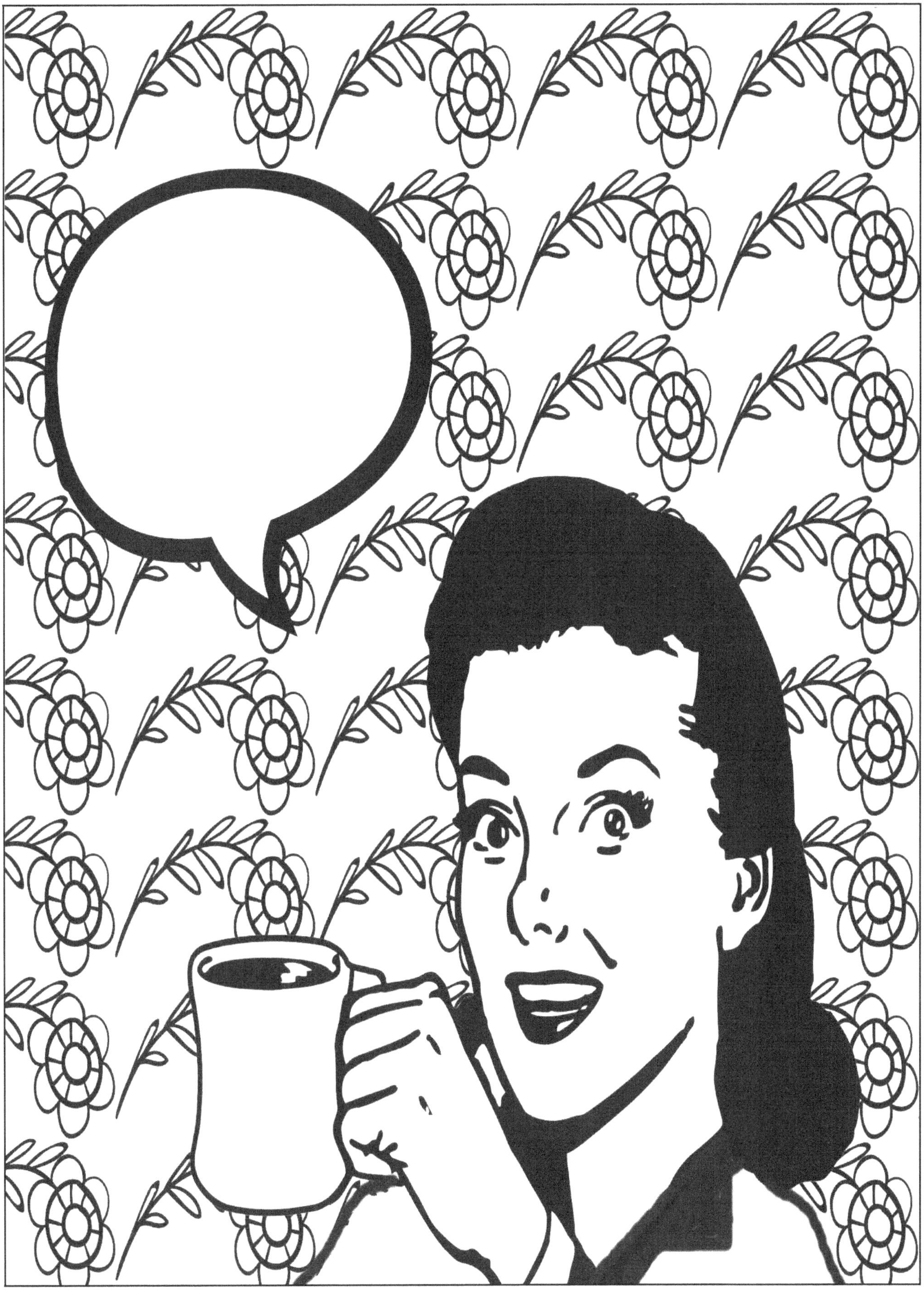

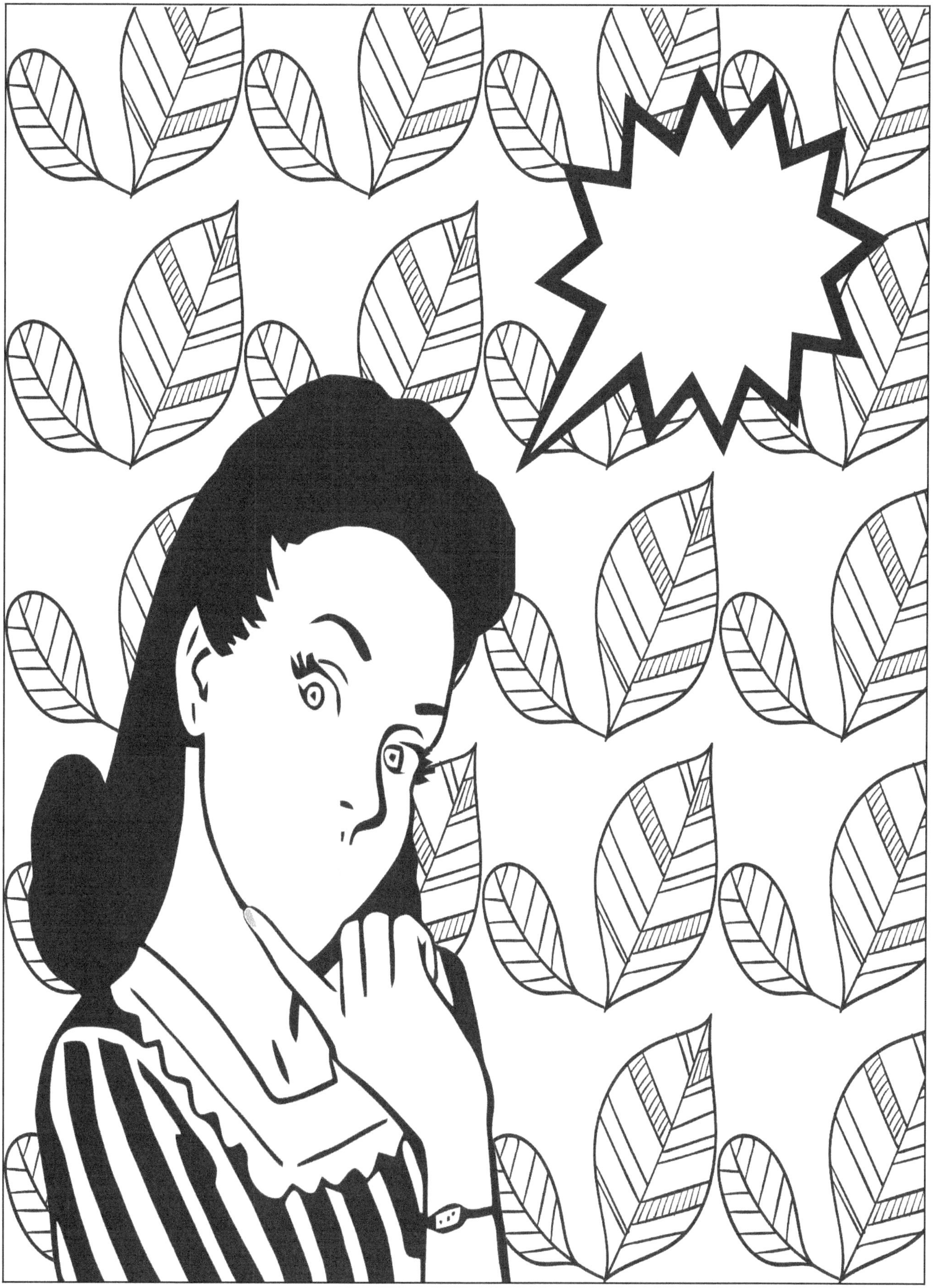

Visit **www.swearwordscoloringbooks.com**
For some more coloring inspiration

www.ingramcontent.com/pod-product-compliance
Lightning Source LLC
Chambersburg PA
CBHW080716190526
45169CB00006B/2397
* 9 7 8 1 5 3 2 9 1 3 5 4 9 *